# THE
# BOOK
# OF
# DAVIDO

Onyeka Nwelue, born in 1988, is a Nigerian scholar,filmmaker, jazz musician and publisher, who has published over 30 books, the most popular being the Crime Fiction Lovers' Awards-winning *The Strangers of Braamfontein*, described by Nobel Laureate, Wole Soyinka, as 'raunchy.'Nwelue was an Academic Visitor to the University of Oxford and Visiting Scholar in the University of Cambridge. He was a Visiting Research Fellow at Ohio University and a Research Associate at the University of Johannesburg. His documentary *The House of Nwapa* was nominated in the Best Documentary category at the 2017 Africa Movie Academy Awards. The next year, Nwelue adapted his novella *Island of Happiness* into an Igbo film, Agwaetiti Obiụtọ, which was nominated in the Best First Feature Film and Best Film in an African Language categories at the 2018 Africa Movie Academy Awards and won the Best Film by a Director at the Newark International Film Festival.

In 2024, his biopic of Emeka Ojukwu, *Other Side of History*, was screened at the Toronto International Film Festival.

Nwelue is the director of Africa Center Mexico.

# THE BOOK OF DAVIDO

## ONYEKA NWELUE

**Abibiman**
Publishing

New York & London

Published in the United Kingdom in 2025 by
Abibiman Publishing
www.abibimanpublishing.com

Abibiman Publishing is registered under
Hudics LLC in the United States and in
the  United Kingdom

ISBN: 978-1-0685027-6-7

This is not a work of fiction.

Cover design by Fred Martins

Printed at Clays UK

## The Women of Biafra Review

The story of Biafra...that should never be forgotten
- **Frederick Forsyth**

Nwelue doesn't shy away from the brutal realities of war. The Biafran War novel has become an established genre within Nigerian literature and known for stories that skillfully depict the visceral sense of war.
- **Brittlepaper Review**

*The Women of Biafra* is a short but highly effective novel. Using plain, straightforward language – peppered with some brilliantly evocative similes – Nwelue vividly portrays the atrocities committed against Biafran civilians by Nigerian troops, and one woman's dogged determination to survive for the sake of her loved ones.
- **Dr. Alice Violett**

*The Women of Biafra* is a captivating and evocative work of fiction set against the tumultuous backdrop of the Nigerian Civil War
- **The Secret Book Review UK**

Onyeka Nwelue's *The Women of Biafra* is a harrowing exploration of the Nigerian Civil War through the eyes of those often overlooked: women. Structured in a dramatic, episodic format, the novel plunges readers into the visceral horrors of conflict, offering a stark and unflinching portrayal of human suffering.

Nwelue's mastery lies in his ability to evoke raw emotion. The closing scene of Part II, "Enemy Territory," is a case in point. The graphic depiction of Mark's mutilated body and Mama Idu's heart-wrenching grief is both shocking and profoundly moving. It sets the tone for a narrative that spares no detail in its exploration of war's brutal realities.

**- The BagusNG Review**

I am pleased that the author took on the challenge of putting this pain into words bevaise the story of their plight needed to be told, to be shared, so that people could learn from such ways.

I was so hooked on this booked.

**- Bwignall**

## The Nigerian Mafia: Mumbai Review

*The Nigerian Mafia Mumbai* by Onyeka Nwelue is a phenomenal book in many regards. It has culture, crime, cult, and lust, all packaged in a unique, original voice of Onyeka Nwelue. It'll make you laugh and smile, until everything fades away in the end.

- **Bombayreads**

Onyeka Nwelue has been a world traveler with long experience in both Lagos and Mumbai. I am deeply impressed with how the author uses the stream of consciousness memoir to impress upon readers just how thoroughly corrupt and yet still somewhat sympathetic Mbadiegwu is.

- **Scintilla Book Review**

I really should read more novels by African authors, this one by prollific Nigerian author Nwelue was only the second I've read this year.

I wasn't entirely sure what to expect of a novel that is titled *Nigerian Mafia: Mumbai* with mentions of Nollywood and Bollywood, the end of the blurb stresses the former concerns rather than the latter: 'The Nigerian Mafia is a tale of violence, drugs, human trafficking, murder and sex.'

- **Anna Bookbel Review**

*The Nigerian Mafia Mumbai*, by Onyeka Nwelue, presents a raw and unflinching account of the lives and experiences of African migrants in Mumbai and other parts of India. Uche's narration is stark, unforgiving, and brutal, offering a compelling insight into their struggles.

–**Suleiman Ahmed is the author of Trouble in Valhalla**

## The Nigerian Mafia: Johannesburg Review

*The Nigerian Mafia: Johannesburg* is a blistering run through a morally corrupt yet interesting man's attempt to find a new life in a new country. An interesting, if extremely short, read.

- **Mail and Guardian Magazine South Africa**

In this very brief episode in the life of Uche - a Nigerian hitman - we are guided through his misadventures in the City of Gold (Johannesburg). After escaping Sao Paulo, Uche finds himself in Jozi where his day-job as a hired killer leads him to run-ins with loan sharks, organised Chinese crime syndicates in Bruma, and the general chaos of life in Yeoville. After a drug-deal gone wrong, Uche flees once again to Cape Town to find peace. While he is temporarily able to achieve this once he meets Kanya - a beautiful, wise young woman who he quickly falls for, the utopia is only fleeting as his life slowly begins to fall into disarray once again.

While the subject matter tackled in this novella is captivating and eye-opening, the story is lacking in focus, and proper character exploration. Uche is a man on the run, unable to settle because of his choice (arguable perhaps) to pursue a life of crime. We see, in him, the quest to settle down and lead a normal life but the underworld of the Nigerian Mafia seems to keep pulling him back whenever he attempts to. Aside from this, the reader is not offered anything deeper as far as understanding Uche's motives. This, to a strong degree, sterilises the story. This insufficient character development also makes the story appear rather rushed and incomplete.

Reading this as a written account of crime syndicates in South Africa will probably increase one's satisfaction with the book. As a novella, due to the superficial way in which the author handles the presentation of characters - including the MP - it falls drastically short of being the truly captivating short read it could be had the author spent more time on it.

- **Thabs, Review Goodreads**

# Strangers of Braamfontein Review

"*The Strangers of Braamfontein* is a perceptive and vigorous tale of people trapped in dire circumstances"

**- Kirkus Reviews.**

'*The Strangers of Braamfontein*' is heavily peopled with characters as dark as the night who are cohabiting in a brutal place where death is cheap. Raw, gritty, fast-paced, this is not a book you can glance through because it will force you to keep turning the pages. It will make you shiver with trepidation. It is such a searing read. This is a book to love.

**- Olukorede S. Yishau, The Lagos Review.**

"*The Strangers of Braamfontein* is one of those crime novels that hits you in the gut and before you can recover another powerful blow is delivered. It's a story of corruption, gangland violence, sex trafficking, modern slavery and murder. All of this is seen from the perspective of the people brutalised, abused and discarded and those profiting and perpetuating their misery."

**- Paul Burke, Crime Fiction Lover.**

"The novel features a colorful and sprawling cast of characters, each motivated by the dictates of a world where survival is in deed for the fittest."

**- ALESIA ALEXANDER, Brittle Paper.**

"There is no downtime with *The Strangers of Braamfontein*. The pacing is fast and is sustained all through to the last page. I like the character Osas, mostly. He represents the hopeful African youth who travels to break out of the dire situation at home. The drug lord Papi is another character I find very interesting, and then there is the prostitute who falls in love with Osas. This is my second time reading the book and I don't trust myself well enough to not come back to it repeatedly."

- **Ikenna Okeh, Author of The Operative.**

"Onyeka Nwelue's *The Strangers of Braamfontein* is timely and urgent, a necessary read, in view of recent happenings in South Africa. Moreover, it is a novel that African migration and diaspora scholars may find relevant in discussing intra-continental migration and its complexities—insofar as they have the appetite for its grisly servings."

- **Uche Umezurike, Author of Double wahala, Double trouble.**

"*The Strangers of Braamfontein* is a portrait of broken dreams. It is a book of piranhas destined for a fatal ending."

- **Miterrand Okorie, Nigerian Abroad.**

"Funny, lively and compelling characters, Onyeka Nwelue's *The Strangers of Braamfontein* is a memorable read. "

–**Jumoke Verissimo, author of A Small Silence**

"*The Strangers Of Braamfontein* holds up a cracked, blood-stained mirror to modern, post-colonial Africa. Tackling themes of xenophobia, homophobia, racism, sex trafficking

and more, *The Strangers Of Braamfontein* lays bare the desperate lengths people will go to in search of a better life.
                                                    - **Megan Thomas, Buzz Mag.**

"*The Strangers of Braamfontein* is a grim, grisly view of post-Apartheid South Africa, and among its wide range of characters there are barely any who aren't morally compromised. But, for all its bleakness, it sizzles with a visceral, pulpy energy."
                                    - **Alastair Mabbott, The Herald of Scotland.**

"If you want a different book, with a spotlight on a world a long way from your own back door, this is well worth a try and will linger in the memory. You can't help but keep your fingers crossed that for some, there is hope and a glimmer of light."
                                                    - **Adrian Magson,**
                            **The author 23 Spy and Crime Thrillers.**

Onyeka's style of writing is straightforward. *The Strangers of Braamfontein* educates you, entertains you and throws harsh realities at your face. The novel portrays a typical 21st century African millennial society that exposes the tyranny of government officials and leaders. It will hook you to the end and keep you hanging on a cliff. No crime fiction comes close to this. This is simply the best I have read in a very long time.
                                                    - **Chidimma Eze.**

*The Strangers of Braamfontein* is a thriller. The very best of them you could possibly find out there. It is realistic and it shocks you to your roots, making you question the things you think you know. The characters are relatable. This is a strong and deeply felt novel. I enjoyed it. I am impressed and hooked and I am sure that many others will say the same of this book.

- Daniella Eze.

*The Strangers of Braamfontein* is a well written book and the plot tells of the depth of the writer's understanding of the human condition in many African mega cities. This is a story with twists and turns that you can never predict. It keeps your heart pacing and you don't realize when you begin to take responsibility for the characters. Onyeka really gets me hooked on this one, and he has to keep this up. I can't wait for his next crime novel.

-Nwodo Henry.

Onyeka Nwelue sets a quick pace in "*The Strangers Of Braamfontein*" as he masterfully narrates the harsh realities that plays out in Braamfontein. This story is set against the backdrop of organized crime in its undiluted forms. The Strangers of Braamfontein is so good. It is a masterpiece and I admit that I have read it more than once.

- Chukwunyere Ejike.

I have never read anything like this written by an African. *The Strangers of Braamfontein* is a great crime tale. I will be glad if many young people read this novel. It will open their eyes to the reality of what life could possibly turn out for an immigrant in a foreign land.

- Francis Ifeanyichukwu Okwara.

## No Crime Novel Comes Close To The Strangers of Braamfontein

Onyeka Nwelue knows what is at stake and he does so well with *The Strangers of Braamfontein* in portraying a 21st century Africa doomed by the sting of corruption, crime and desperation. This novel puts the spotlight on the ugly influence of intimidation, mismanagement of power by government officials and the leaders. especially their complicity in the rate at which crime and illegality attracts young people who hold onto the "get rich quick" syndrome.

Quite remarkable is the writer's figurative attempt to depict the life of drug dealing in all of its grandeur and danger, leading us on with his engaging narrative through scenes after scenes of violence, sex and betrayal.

I like his style of writing. It is straightforward. It makes you take a dive in from the first pages and excites you from the onset and all through the entire pages of the book, educating you, entertaining you and throwing harsh realities at your face. Onyeka invested well enough in vibrant characters depicting them as passionate and real. It is with this same real passion that Onyeka have written and presented this book. It will hook you to the end and keep you hanging on a cliff. No crime fiction comes close to this. This is simply the best I have read in a very long time.

-Chidimma Eze.

# This Is Onyeka's Perfect Outing As a Writer

*The strangers of Braamfontein* is a thriller, the very best of them you could possibly find out there. It is realistic and it shocks you to your roots, making you question the things you think you know. The action takes your breath away; you always want to know what happens next to your favourite character. It is the social and moral oddity that captures me about this book and Onyeka did a really great job in highlighting these things in ways that gets the plot going forward. Ingenious.

The characters are relatable. I mean if you have ever had an experience with the rough side of things in Africa, you will easily relate with the characters and the worlds in which they find themselves. I like it that Onyeka entertains us within surroundings that we can identify. Prostitution, drugs, human trafficking have done so much damage to societies in Africa and this is the main focus of the book. We also see it in the book that the governments of affected societies are doing nothing to stop these things. I find this to be honest and courageous of the writer and such values ought to be recognized.

The world that the writer painted in this book is a harsh one. In it, only the strongest survive. It is a jungle. A place where A world recognized for its greed, violence, betrayal, lust and ruthless use of power. Yet it is the reality that we should be strong enough to confront. It is the world of millions of people, their reality.

This is a strong and deeply felt novel. I enjoyed it. I am impressed and hooked and I am sure that many others will say the same of this book.

- Daniella Eze.

# Nwelue's Breakthrough As a Writer Is This Crime Novel

*The Strangers of Braamfontein* is a well written book and the plot tells of the depth of the writer's understanding of the human condition in many African mega cities. His depiction of Braamfontein is no different from the realities of many others in Nairobi or Lagos or any other major African metropolitan cities where poverty is and desperation stares you in the face. Onyeka Nwelue must be a master of suspense to have achieved what he did with this book. I began reading it and it swept me off. There is hardly anything about it that isn't familiar to an observant eye. It mirrors the human condition, a testament to how easily our humanity can be eroded when we dwell for too long with hunger and desperation.

I am drawn to the character, Osas. He had left Nigeria with the hope of making it big n South Africa. But to his surprise he had exchanged one desperate level for another. Life in South Africa takes him through a story of betrayal, love, lust, and fear, all of which beams and wanes at every turn of Osas' life and with the interaction he has with every other characters. Oh, and as for other characters, they are as indepth as Osas. I don't exactly like thinking about the Chamai character. He breaks my heart. I wish things have ended up differently for him with the closeted homosexual Chike. Btu instead, Chike takes advantage of his desperation and things ended up with Chamai the way it did. Really breaks my heart.

This is a story with twists and turns that you can never predict. It keeps your heart pacing and you don't realize when you begin to take responsibility for the characters. Onyeka really gets me hooked on this one, and he has to keep this up. I can't wait for his next crime novel.

- **Nwodo Henry.**

## The Strangers of Braamfontein Is So Good

From the very beginning, Onyeka Nwelue sets a quick pace in "*The Strangers Of Braamfontein*" as he masterfully narrates the harsh realities that plays out in Braamfontein. This story is set against the backdrop of organized crime in its undiluted forms. I noticed my eyes were wet and my heart beat faster than usual as I read Ruth narrating her story to her girls, yes her girls.

I don't know why I am more drawn to the character of Ruth and her girls. Every time, there are stories of girls trafficked out of African countries by prostitution rings, sometimes unwillingly and sometimes willingly. This is one book that treats the situation in a way that entertains, questions and enlightens the reader. I am sure it should be a reference point whenever issues of trafficking and organized crime is being discussed.

I had imagined a turn of events when I got to that point where the prostitute, April, gets pregnant for Osas, the drug dealer, who also has a secret thing going with April's boss, Ruth. But then it had turned out differently and I had been left wondering how sleek Onyeka Nwelue is with spinning his plot in such a way that made a fool of me in trying to be predictive. The Strangers of Braamfontein is so good. It is a masterpiece and I admit that I have read it more than once.

- Chukwunyere Ejike.

## The Strangers of Braamfontein
## Is a Great Crime Tale

My favorite character is the young Nigerian, Osas, who travels to Braamfontein so as to make it big. His story is an honest depiction of the fate of millions of Nigerians and Africans who travel overseas in the hope of better lives and success. Most times they don't relate their experiences and we don't know what life for them abroad is. But with *The Strangers of Braamfontein*, we can see realities play before our eyes and we can enjoy these realities as the entertainment that they are.

I have never read anything like this written by an African. It takes a certain level of boldness to write about issues like this in such a detailed manner. Maybe this is what writing should be, and if we can look at our world as closely as Onyeka Nwelue is making us do with this book, then we can begin to have honest conversations that are channeled towards making better societies for ourselves.

The character, Papi, is another one I like. He is a clear example of what happens when we become too comfortable in predatory worlds. The jungle is what it is, and even predators could be preyed upon. I like the fact that Nwelue portrays that if ever a place have a reputation for crime, it is so because people in high places who are supposed to protect the interests of the people who elected them there are beneficiaries of the institutionalized rot. We see this with the policemen who are on the payroll of Papi. I love what Nwelue did with this. I am impressed.

I will be glad if many young people read this novel. It will open their eyes to the reality of what life could possibly turn out for an immigrant in a foreign land.

- Francis Ifeanyichukwu Okwara.

"...Like a persistent itch that only goes away by scratching, it is hard to ignore this writer."

- Eromo Egbejule, The Guardian (UK)

"The literary world can do with more babies from the bassinet of "The Strangers of Braamfontein"!"

- Wole Soyinka, Nobel Laureate.

## Praise for Burnt

"Spiders, snakes, disco, paternal violence, Jacques Brel, literary Lagos, Africans in Europe - it's a breathless series of vignettes, anecdotes and narratives we meet in Onyeka Nwelue's Burnt, the whole related fast in rapidly successive moments. The voice is direct, talking you through events. Sometimes it assumes the personal, sometimes it shifts through the overheard and imagined. It is very much a multi-cultural world, the book itself a city of sorts where every window is open. So you keep watching and listening."

- George Szirtes, author of The Slant Door (1979)

"Onyeka Nwelue has written himself. These poems are vintage Onyeka: raw, honest and beautiful. Always edgy."

- Bwesigye bwa Mwesigir,
author of Fables Out of Nyanja

"Daringly different and unarguably exquisite, these poems posses unseen but felt arm that leads your entire being through boulevards decorated with brilliant narratives that keep you walking without stopping, but yearning for more. Here is a delectable oeuvre that resonates. One more feather on OnyekaNwelue's baronial hat. Yes."

- Echezonachukwu Nduka,
author of Echoes of Sentiments

"Sublime, strange and experimental. I read Burnt with a great admiration for Onyeka Nwelue. Each flow, each sentence, each line has something tasteless about it, yet is bewitching."

**- Chika Onyenezi, author of Sea Lavender**

*This book is dedicated to*
*Asa Asika, for being...*

# CONTENTS

# 1

## THE BIRTH OF DAVID

ONYEKA NWELUE

In the beginning, there was rhythm.

The world was akin to the first note of a symphony—full of promise, rhythm, and resonance.

David Adedeji Adeleke entered the world, the youngest of five siblings, into a family where affluence and ambition were the cornerstones. His father, Adedeji Adeleke, a Nigerian business magnate, and his mother, Veronica Adeleke, a university lecturer, provided a nurturing environment that balanced discipline with encouragement. They both imbued him with a love for knowledge and culture. Yet, within Davido stirred a different melody—a yearning for beats, rhythms, and the soulful strains of music that would later define his destiny.

Not the kind that merely pulses through speakers, but a primordial cadence that resonates in the marrow of one's bones—a beat that predates language, a melody that whispers the secrets of the universe. It is in this eternal rhythm that our story finds its genesis.

On November 21, 1992, in the heart of Atlanta, a city steeped in musical heritage, a child was born: David Adedeji Adeleke

From the outset, David's life was a symphony of contrasts. Raised amidst the opulence of Lagos and the cultural mosaic of Atlanta, he was a child of two worlds: tradition and modernity. The bustling streets of Lagos, with their cacophony of sounds, served as his early orchestra. From the rhythmic chants of street vendors to the harmonious hymns of church choirs, every sound was a note in his burgeoning musical score. This bicultural upbringing would later infuse his music with a distinctive blend of African rhythms and Western influences, setting the stage for a career that would transcend borders.

David's formative years were marked by a deep-seated passion for music. While attending the British International School in Lagos, he exhibited an affinity for sound that went beyond mere appreciation. At 16, he returned to the United States to study Business Administration at Oakwood University in Alabama. However, the call of music proved irresistible. He poured his money into musical gear and started making beats, setting the stage for a prolific career.

As I reflect upon David's early journey, I am reminded of my own path—a journey marked by a relentless pursuit of creative expression. Born in Ezeoke Nsu, Imo State, Nigeria, I was shaped in my formative years by literature and storytelling. Like David, I found myself at the crossroads of tradition and innovation, seeking to carve a niche in a world that often resists the unconventional.

In Nigerian music, few stories resonate as profoundly as that of Davido. His father envisioned a conventional path for his children: academic excellence leading to roles in the family's expansive business empire. This vision was deeply rooted in the family's values, with education being paramount.

However, from an early age, Davido exhibited a passion for music that diverged from his family's expectations. While attending Oakwood University in Alabama, he invested in musical equipment and began crafting beats, collaborating with his cousins in a group called KB International. This burgeoning interest soon took precedence over his studies, leading him to drop out and relocate to London to hone his vocal skills.

Upon returning to Nigeria in 2011, Davido's commitment to music intensified. He secretly set up a studio in his room, recording tracks during the day while his father was at work, keeping musical pursuits hidden. This secrecy was necessary, as his father was initially unaware of his son's foray into music. Davido later revealed, "My dad didn't know I was a musician till about two years after I started recording."

The revelation of Davido's musical endeavors was met with significant resistance. His father, emphasizing the importance of education, took drastic measures to deter him. In interviews, Davido recounted instances where his father would cancel his shows and even arrest promoters to prevent him from performing. He once stated, "If he saw my face on a billboard, he'd arrest everybody at that show!"

Despite these challenges, Davido remained undeterred. In 2011, he released his debut single, "Back When," featuring Naeto C, which garnered significant attention. However, it was his follow-up track, "Dami Duro", a track that resonated across Nigeria and beyond, that catapulted him into the limelight, solidifying his status as a rising star in the Nigerian music scene. The song's success was a turning point, compelling his father to reconsider his stance. Recognizing his son's potential, Adedeji Adeleke took steps to support his career. He bought Davido out of his first professional recording contract to ensure he owned 100% of his music masters.

Furthermore, to reconcile his desire for his son to complete his education with Davido's musical ambitions, Adedeji Adeleke offered a compromise. He promised to build a world-class studio for Davido and fund his music videos, provided he returned to university. Davido agreed, and enrolled at Babcock University, where he eventually graduated with a degree in music.

This journey underscores that Davido's success was not handed to him on a silver platter. He navigated familial expectations, societal pressures, and personal challenges, demonstrating resilience and dedication to his craft. Today, his story serves as an inspiration, illustrating that with passion and perseverance, one can carve a unique path, even when it diverges from traditional expectations.

It was in that same 2011 that our paths converged in a serendipitous encounter that would leave an indelible mark on my perception of artistry. I met David in Lagos, a city that pulsates with creative energy. At the time, I was immersed in literature and film, exploring narratives that challenged societal norms. David, with his infectious charisma and unwavering determination, embodied the spirit of a new generation of artists—unapologetically authentic and fiercely innovative.

In the heart of Lagos, where the city's rhythm is set by the cacophony of honking danfos and the melodic calls of street vendors, our paths crossed in a moment that felt orchestrated by fate itself. 2011 was a year that marked a turning point in both our lives.

I had just returned from a literary tour, my mind brimming with stories and my heart yearning for new artistic collaborations. The city was alive with creative energy, and I found myself drawn to the vibrant music scene that was redefining Nigeria's cultural landscape.

One evening, at a mutual friend's gathering in Lekki, I was introduced to a young man whose presence was quietly commanding and was marked by a calm confidence that drew attention without demanding it. Dressed casually, with a cap tilted slightly to the side and a smile that exuded warmth, he extended his hand and said, "I'm David."

There was an immediate connection, a shared understanding between two artists passionate about their crafts. We spoke at length about music, literature, and the power of storytelling. David's knowledge of diverse musical genres and his appreciation for lyrical depth impressed me. He spoke of his desire to create music that resonated with people, that told authentic Nigerian stories with a global appeal.

In the weeks that followed, our paths continued to intersect. I visited his makeshift studio, a modest room transformed into a creative haven filled with recording equipment, scribbled lyrics, and an air of relentless ambition. There, I witnessed firsthand the dedication and discipline that belied his age. He would spend hours perfecting beats, experimenting with melodies, and refining his lyrics.

One particular session stands out in my memory. David was working on a track that would later become one of his early hits. As he played the beat and sang the chorus, I was struck by the authenticity and raw emotion in his voice. It was clear that he was not just creating music; he was pouring his soul into every note.

Our interactions deepened my appreciation for the emerging Nigerian music scene and its potential to influence global culture. David's journey mirrored my own in many ways—a pursuit of artistic excellence, a commitment to authenticity, and a desire to impact society through our respective crafts.

As I reflect on that period, I am reminded of the words of Wole Soyinka, who once said, "The greatest threat to freedom is the absence of criticism." David welcomed constructive feedback, constantly seeking ways to improve and evolve as an artist. His openness to growth and his unwavering work ethic were testaments to his future success.

In the early stages of his career, Davido faced significant criticism regarding his vocal style. His distinctive deep, raspy voice, often described as "hazy" or "husky," became a focal point for detractors. Social media trolls mockingly dubbed him "frog voice," attempting to undermine his credibility as a vocalist.

Despite these critiques, Davido remained undeterred. He acknowledged the challenges posed by his vocal timbre, especially during performances when he would sometimes lose his voice. Medical professionals advised him to limit nonessential speaking to preserve his vocal cords. Reflecting on these experiences, Davido shared:

"Because my voice is already husky, when my voice goes, it's so annoying. I like to express myself and I speak a lot, so when I can't talk, it's annoying."

Rather than allowing these obstacles to hinder his progress, Davido embraced his unique voice, turning what many perceived as a weakness into a defining strength. His commitment to his craft and resilience in the face of adversity contributed to his rise as one of Africa's leading music artists.

Over time, public perception shifted. His performances, notably at venues like the O2 Arena, showcased his growth as an artist and silenced many of his early critics. The very voice that was once a subject of ridicule became emblematic of his authenticity and passion.

Davido's journey underscores the importance of self-belief and perseverance. By confronting criticism head-on and staying true to his artistic vision, he transformed challenges into milestones, solidifying his place in the global music landscape.

Meeting Davido was more than a chance encounter; it was the beginning of a journey that would see a young man rise to become one of Africa's most influential musicians. His story is one of passion, perseverance, and the transformative power of art. As I continue to chronicle his life and career, I am inspired by the impact he has made and the legacy he continues to build.

David's ascent was not merely a personal triumph but the genesis of a movement. In 2016, he founded Davido Music Worldwide (DMW), a record label that would become a launchpad for emerging talents like Mayorkun and Peruzzi. Through DMW, David cultivated a community that celebrated creativity and collaboration, fostering an environment where artists could thrive.

Today, Davido stands as a luminary in the global music industry, his influence extending beyond the realm of entertainment. His philanthropic endeavors, including the establishment of the Davido Music Worldwide Foundation, underscore a commitment to social responsibility. Through initiatives aimed at improving education and healthcare in Nigeria, he leverages his platform to effect meaningful change.

Davido's birth was more than the arrival of a child; it was the inception of a force that would redefine the contours of African music. His journey, marked by resilience and innovation, serves as a testament to the transformative power of art. As I continue to navigate my own creative pursuits, I find inspiration in Davido's story—a narrative that affirms the boundless possibilities that emerge when passion meets purpose.

# 2

. . . .

# LORD OF
# ATLANTA

In the Peach State of the American South, where magnolias bloom and hip-hop beats pulse through the humid air, a young Davido was born. In the symphony of his life, Atlanta served as the overture—a city where the rhythms of the American South harmonized with the beats of West Africa. Born in Atlanta's Northside Hospital, Davido's early years were steeped in the rich musical heritage of the city and its cultural fusion would serve as the backdrop for the formative years of a boy destined to become an Afrobeats luminary.

Though his roots were firmly planted in Nigerian soil, Davido's early life was a transatlantic dance between continents. His parents, recognizing the value of both worlds, ensured he spent his summers in Atlanta's Sandy Springs and Norcross neighborhoods. These annual pilgrimages exposed him to the vibrant tapestry of Southern hip-hop, a genre that would later intertwine with his African musical sensibilities.

At 16, Davido enrolled at Oakwood University in Alabama, a historically Black institution. It was here that his passion for music ignited. A chance encounter with a dorm neighbor who had a makeshift studio introduced him to the world of music production. Investing in his own equipment, Davido began crafting beats and recording tracks, laying the foundation for his future career.

Despite his burgeoning interest in music, academic challenges loomed. His grades suffered, leading to his departure from Oakwood. Undeterred, Davido relocated to Atlanta, immersing himself in the city's dynamic music scene. While underaged, he used his older brother's ID to access clubs as he absorbed the rhythms and rhymes of local artists, further shaping his musical identity.

Atlanta's streets pulsed with the energy of crunk, trap, and R&B. Artists like Lil Jon, T.I., and OutKast dominated the airwaves, their beats and rhymes shaping the city's sonic landscape. Davido absorbed these influences, internalizing the swagger and cadence of Southern hip-hop. Yet, his Nigerian heritage remained a constant presence, with the melodies of D'banj and Don Jazzy echoing in his ears.

This duality—Atlanta's gritty beats and Nigeria's rhythmic melodies—became the hallmark of Davido's sound. His music emerged as a fusion of these worlds, blending the percussive elements of Afrobeats with the lyrical flow of American hip-hop. This synthesis was not merely a stylistic choice but a reflection of his bicultural identity.

In the early 2010s, amidst the vibrant musical landscapes of Atlanta and Lagos, a new force was emerging in the Nigerian music scene: HKN Gang. Founded by Davido and his elder brother, Adewale Adeleke, HKN—an acronym for "Hakan," a Turkish word meaning "ruler"—

was more than just a record label; it was a familial enterprise rooted in shared dreams and musical passion.

Atlanta, Georgia played a pivotal role in shaping the musical aspirations of the Adeleke family. Davido was immersed in the city's dynamic music culture from a young age. His cousins, B-Red (Adebayo Adeleke) and Sina Rambo (Shina Adeleke), also shared this environment, fostering a shared dream to make it in the music industry. Their time in Atlanta wasn't just about absorbing musical influences; it was about laying the groundwork for what would become HKN Gang.

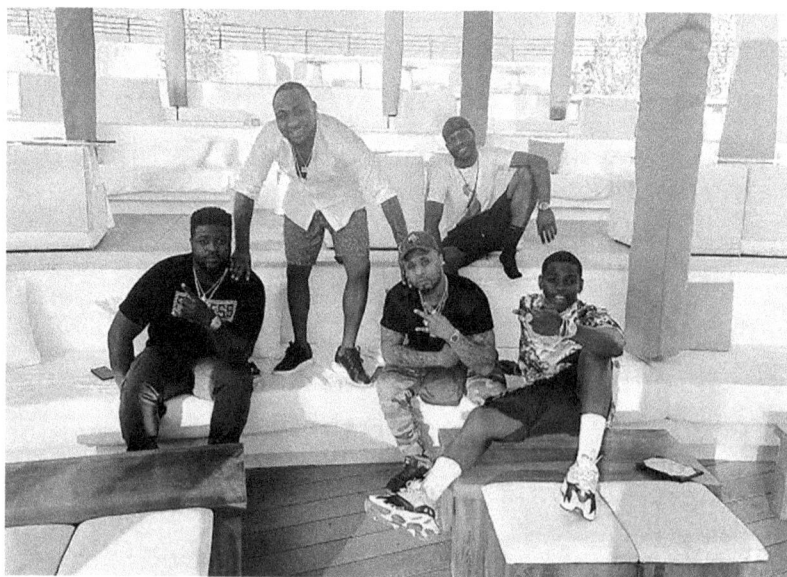

The trio's collaboration began in earnest during their time in Atlanta. They experimented with sounds, wrote songs, and performed together, honing their craft and building a cohesive musical identity. This period was marked by a shared vision: to create music that resonated both locally and internationally. Their synergy was evident in their performances and recordings, setting the stage for their eventual move to Nigeria to fully pursue their musical careers.

Recognizing the numerous opportunities in Nigeria's music industry, Davido, B-Red, and Sina Rambo relocated to Lagos. This move was strategic, aiming to tap into the vibrant Afrobeats scene and connect with a broader audience. In Lagos, they officially established HKN Gang, with Davido as the frontman. The label quickly gained traction, releasing hits that blended Western musical elements with African rhythms.

Despite their early successes, HKN Gang faced internal challenges. Reports surfaced of tensions between Davido and his cousins, B-Red and Sina Rambo, stemming from concerns about promotion and artistic direction. In 2013, a notable incident occurred in Atlanta, where a disagreement escalated into a physical altercation, highlighting the tension within the group. These challenges tested the resilience of HKN Gang, prompting reflections on leadership and collaboration within the label.

While internal dynamics shifted, the impact of HKN Gang on the Nigerian music industry remained significant. The label served as a launchpad for Davido's illustrious career and provided a platform for other artists to showcase their talents. The experiences and lessons from HKN Gang informed Davido's future endeavors, including the establishment of his subsequent label, Davido Music Worldwide (DMW), in 2016.

Davido's time in Atlanta also exposed him to the challenges of straddling two cultures. In interviews, he has spoken about the complexities of his identity, stating, "You're from where your parents are from." This acknowledgment of his Nigerian roots, despite his American birth, underscores the internal conflict and eventual reconciliation that defined his early years.

The city's vibrant music scene provided Davido with opportunities to hone his craft. Collaborations with local artists and exposure to diverse musical styles enriched his artistic palette. These experiences laid the foundation for his debut album which showcased his ability to seamlessly integrate different genres.

Atlanta's influence extended beyond music. The city's culture of resilience and innovation inspired Davido to carve his own path in the industry. He embraced the entrepreneurial spirit of Atlanta's music scene, establishing his own label and nurturing emerging talents. This commitment to fostering growth within the industry reflects the values he absorbed during his formative years in the city.

In essence, Atlanta served as both a crucible and a canvas for Davido. It was where he confronted the complexities of his identity, embraced the richness of his heritage, and cultivated the sound that would propel him to global stardom. The city's influence is indelibly etched into his music, a testament to the transformative power of cultural convergence.

Davido's journey was not without obstacles. Skepticism surrounded his musical aspirations, with many attributing his opportunities to his family's wealth. He recalled, "What was difficult for me was coming from a very wealthy background. Everybody just thought , 'Nah, his dad... This is money.'"

Determined to prove his merit, Davido distanced himself from his family's affluence, choosing instead to hone his craft independently. He spent countless hours in studios, collaborating with local artists and refining his sound. His dedication culminated in the release of his debut album, "Omo Baba Olowo," in 2012, a project that showcased his unique blend of Afrobeat and hip-hop.

Davido's time in Atlanta was instrumental in shaping his identity as a global Afrobeats ambassador. The city's musical diversity and cultural richness provided a fertile ground for experimentation and growth. By integrating the soulful melodies of African music with the gritty beats of Southern hip-hop, he crafted a sound that resonated across continents.

His experiences in Atlanta also instilled in him a deep appreciation for collaboration and cultural exchange. These values would later manifest in his numerous international collaborations, further cementing his status as a bridge between African music and the global stage.

Davido's connection to Atlanta was not merely geographical. It was in this city that he first encountered the pulsating beats and lyrical prowess that defined Southern hip-hop. These experiences, combined with his Nigerian heritage, created a unique fusion of sounds that would become the hallmark of his music.

Simultaneously, Davido remained deeply connected to Nigerian music, and this duality—melding Southern hip-hop with African rhythms—became the cornerstone of his sound, reflecting his bicultural identity and global perspective.

This chapter, "Lord of Atlanta", encapsulates Davido's mastery over the cultural and musical landscapes that shaped him. In a way like a modern-day Hercules, he navigated the complexities of dual heritage, forging a path that honored both his American birthplace and Nigerian roots. His ability to seamlessly blend these influences speaks to his versatility and artistic vision.

Moreover, Davido's experiences in Atlanta were instrumental in his development as a global Afrobeats ambassador. The city's diverse musical environment provided a fertile ground for experimentation, allowing him to refine his sound and broaden his appeal. This foundation enabled him to bridge cultural divides, bringing African music to international audiences and solidifying his status as a global icon.

In essence, Atlanta was not just a backdrop in Davido's story—it was a crucible that forged his identity and artistry. The city's influence permeates his music, infusing it with a richness and depth that resonates with audiences worldwide. As the "Lord of Atlanta," Davido stands as a testament to the power of cultural fusion and the boundless possibilities it offers to those who dare to embrace it.

# 3

. . . .

# DANCING
# IN THE
# FIREHOUSE

Before the global ascension of Afrobeats, Nigeria's music industry was a vibrant mosaic of traditional rhythms and emerging contemporary sounds. The early 2000s witnessed a fusion of indigenous genres like Highlife, Fuji, and Juju with Western influences, leading to the birth of a unique Nigerian pop sound. Artists such as 2Baba (formerly 2Face Idibia), D'banj, and P-Square became trailblazers, blending local languages and themes with R&B and hip-hop elements. This era was characterized by the rise of independent labels and a burgeoning youth-driven market, setting the stage for Nigeria's music to gain international recognition. The introduction of MTV Base Africa in 2005 further amplified the reach of Nigerian artists, providing a platform for their music videos and increasing their visibility across the continent.

Amidst this dynamic musical evolution, Asa Asika emerged as a pivotal figure in shaping the industry's trajectory. Born on August 14, 1990, in Lagos, Nigeria, Asa was immersed in the entertainment world from a young age. His uncle, Obi Asika, co-founded Storm Records, a label instrumental in shaping Nigeria's contemporary music scene. By sixteen, Asa was already organizing club appearances and promo events for artists like Naeto C, Ikechukwu, and Sasha P. Asa's early immersion in this environment, coupled with his innate acumen, saw him managing artists like YQ and organizing events even before his twenties. It also included managing a student rap group called Bonafide during his high school years at White Sands School, showcasing his innate ability to spot and nurture talent.

His early exposure to event management and artist promotion provided him with invaluable experience in understanding the intricacies of the music business. Asa's role at Storm Records extended beyond promotions; he was actively involved in talent management, A&R (Artists and Repertoire), and strategic planning, contributing to the label's success in nurturing and promoting Nigerian artists.

Asa Asika's tenure at Storm Records coincided with a transformative period in Nigeria's music industry. His hands-on approach and innovative strategies played a significant role in elevating the profiles of the label's artists, facilitating collaborations, and expanding their reach both locally and internationally. Asa's early experiences at Storm Records laid the foundation for his future endeavors, including co-founding The Plug, a multifaceted entertainment company, and managing the career of global Afrobeats superstar Davido.

In the grand narrative of Afrobeats, where dreams often dissolve into the din, rhythms intertwine and destinies converge, a serendipitous meeting between two prodigious talents would influence the course of Afrobeats history. Davido, the Atlanta-born scion with a penchant for pulsating rhythms, and Asa Asika, the Lagos-bred luminary with an ear finely tuned to the cadence of the streets, found their paths entwined in a narrative reminiscent of ancient epics.

In retrospect, Asa Asika's contributions during his formative years at Storm Records were instrumental in shaping the modern Nigerian music industry. His ability to identify talent, coupled with his strategic acumen, not only propelled the careers of individual artists but also influenced the industry's structure, paving the way for the global success of Afrobeats.

Davido and Asa's paths crossed in the corridors of academia. Asa attended White Sands School, while Davido was at the British International School (BIS). Their mutual friends, who moved between these institutions, facilitated their introduction. Asa recalled, "We had a few of those kinds of friends. We had mutual awareness. I remember hearing about a guy named David that used to make music."

At the time, Davido was primarily interested in music production. However, Asa recognized his potential as a performer. Their collaboration began in earnest when Davido decided to pursue a career as an artist, leading to the creation of his debut single, "Back When," featuring Naeto C—Asa's cousin and a respected rapper in his own right. This track, a harmonious blend of Davido's melodic sensibilities and Naeto C's lyrical prowess, resonated with audiences, signaling the arrival of a new force in the industry.

Building on this momentum, the duo embarked on creating "Dami Duro," a track that would catapult Davido into superstardom. Released on October 30, 2011, the song was a bold declaration of intent, with Davido asserting his place in the musical pantheon. Few songs have etched themselves into the collective consciousness as indelibly as Davido's "Dami Duro." Released on October 30, 2011, as the second single from his debut album Omo Baba Olowo, this track was more than just a catchy tune—it was a bold declaration of intent, a fusion of personal narrative and cultural zeitgeist that resonated across demographics.

The inception of "Dami Duro" was rooted in a personal encounter. Davido revealed that an incident with the Nigerian police served as the catalyst for the song's creation. This experience, emblematic of the challenges faced by many young Nigerians, inspired him to channel his frustration and determination into music.

Collaborating with producer Shizzi, Davido crafted a track that seamlessly blended Afrobeat rhythms with contemporary pop sensibilities. The song's production was a collaborative effort, with Davido contributing to the beats and melodies, showcasing his multifaceted talent.

At its core, "Dami Duro" is a proclamation of self-assurance and resilience. The title, which translates to "You can't stop me" in Yoruba, encapsulates the song's central theme: an unwavering determination to succeed despite obstacles. Davido's lyrics, delivered in a mix of English and Yoruba, reflecting his dual cultural identityand the broader aspirations of a generation seeking to redefine success on their terms.

Upon its release, "Dami Duro" quickly ascended the charts, capturing the attention of both fans and industry insiders. The song's infectious rhythm and relatable message struck a chord, propelling Davido into the spotlight. Its popularity extended beyond the music scene; notably, former Oyo State governor Abiola Ajimobi was seen singing the song during a public event, underscoring its widespread appeal.

The accompanying music video, directed by Clarence Peters, further amplified the song's reach. Its vibrant visuals and dynamic storytelling complemented the track's energy, earning accolades such as Most Gifted Newcomer Video of the Year at the 2012 Channel O Music Video Awards.

"Dami Duro" was more than just a hit single; it was the launchpad for Davido's illustrious career. The song's success validated his decision to pursue music, even in the face of initial skepticism from his family. In interviews, Davido recounted how the track's widespread acclaim, including being the ringtone of Nigeria's president at the time, helped shift perceptions and garner support from his father.

Following "Dami Duro," Davido continued to build on his momentum, releasing a series of successful tracks and albums that solidified his status as a leading figure in the Afrobeats movement. The song's influence also paved the way for collaborations with international artists and expanded his reach beyond Nigeria's borders.

Today, "Dami Duro" stands as a seminal work in Davido's discography and a landmark in Nigerian pop culture. Its fusion of personal narrative, cultural commentary, and musical innovation set a new standard for artists in the region. The song's enduring popularity is a testament to its resonance and the universality of its message: a celebration of ambition, resilience, and the unyielding spirit of youth.

In retrospect, "Dami Duro" was not just a song—it was a movement, a clarion call for a generation ready to assert its voice and redefine the narrative. Through this track, Davido didn't just announce his arrival; he heralded a new era in African music.

As their collaboration flourished, so did the complexities of their professional relationship. Despite their burgeoning success, the pressures of the industry led to a professional split in 2012. Asa went on to establish StarGaze Management Company in 2013, managing artists like Naeto C, BOJ, and Ayo Jay. In 2016, he co-founded

The Plug Entertainment with Bizzle Osikoya, further solidifying his influence in the music industry.

Their mutual respect however, remained intact. In 2017, recognizing the synergy they had built, Davido and Asa reunited professionally. Under Asa's management, Davido released chart-topping hits like "If" and "Fall," marking a new era in his career. Their partnership, rooted in mutual respect and shared vision, continues to shape the trajectory of Afrobeats on the global stage.

The alliance between Davido and Asa Asika stands as a testament to the transformative power of collaboration. Their journey, marked by innovation, resilience, and a shared vision, not only shaped their individual trajectories but also left an indelible mark on the global music

# 4

....

# MUSIC IS
# MAGIC

In the realm of human experience, music stands as a profound and mystical force, weaving its magic into the fabric of our lives. Like the sirens of Greek mythology, music's melodies and harmonies beckon us, entrancing our senses and transporting us to realms both familiar and unknown. This enchanting art form has been the subject of fascination across cultures and centuries, with many regarding it as a form of magic that transcends the mundane.. In Nigeria and around the world, this sentiment is echoed by fans and celebrities alike, who view music as a conduit for healing, connection, and transformation.

Internationally, many artists and fans perceive music as a transformative force. Michael Jackson, often referred to as the "King of Pop," described his creative process as an endeavour to "create magic," aiming to produce something so unexpected that it captivates audiences.

Similarly, Joe Jonas, in discussing his solo album "Music for People Who Believe in Love," emphasized how music served as a healing tool during the lowest point in his life, allowing him to process emotions and connect with others on a profound level.

Renowned Indian singer, Rekha Bhardwaj highlighted the unique connection live music fosters between performers and audiences, describing it as an "instant connection" that technology cannot replicate.

In Nigeria, music is deeply woven into the fabric of daily life, serving not just as entertainment but as a spiritual and communal experience. Traditional performances like the

Tiv people's Kwagh-Hir combine music, dance, and storytelling to convey moral lessons and cultural values, embodying the belief that music holds a magical quality that can educate and unite communities.

Contemporary Nigerian artists continue this tradition. Beautiful Nubia, for instance, uses his music to promote social reform and communal harmony, crafting songs that resonate with universal truths and advocate for a balanced society.

In the realm of Afrobeats, artists like Rema have faced both acclaim and controversy, with some attributing their captivating performances to mystical influences, reflecting the genre's powerful impact on listeners.

Fans worldwide share personal stories of how music has provided comfort and inspiration. Social media platforms are replete with testimonies of individuals who turn to music during challenging times, finding solace in lyrics and melodies that resonate with their experiences. Music has been a profound and multifaceted influence in my life, shaping my identity, creative pursuits, and worldview. From my early years in Ezeoke Nsu, Imo State, Nigeria, I was immersed in a rich collection of sounds that sparked a lifelong passion for the arts.

Across cultures and generations, music is celebrated for its magical qualities—its ability to heal, to connect, and to inspire. Whether through traditional performances in Nigeria or global pop phenomena, music continues to be a powerful force that transcends the ordinary, touching the very essence of the human spirit.

My formal exploration of music began with academic studies in Sociology and Anthropology at the University of Nigeria, Nsukka, which provided a foundational understanding of cultural expressions. This academic journey led me to the Prague Film School in the Czech Republic, where I studied Directing, and later to Berklee College of Music in Boston, where I delved into the Business of Music. These experiences broadened my perspective on the global music industry and deepened my appreciation for the interplay between music and culture.

Music's therapeutic power became particularly evident during a challenging period in my life. While undergoing psychiatric treatment, I channelled my experiences into the creation of my debut world music single, "Break Your Heart." This song, produced by Eternal Nnamdi Mbamara (aka Eternal Africa) and released by Walboomers Music, served as a cathartic outlet and a testament to music's ability to heal and transform.

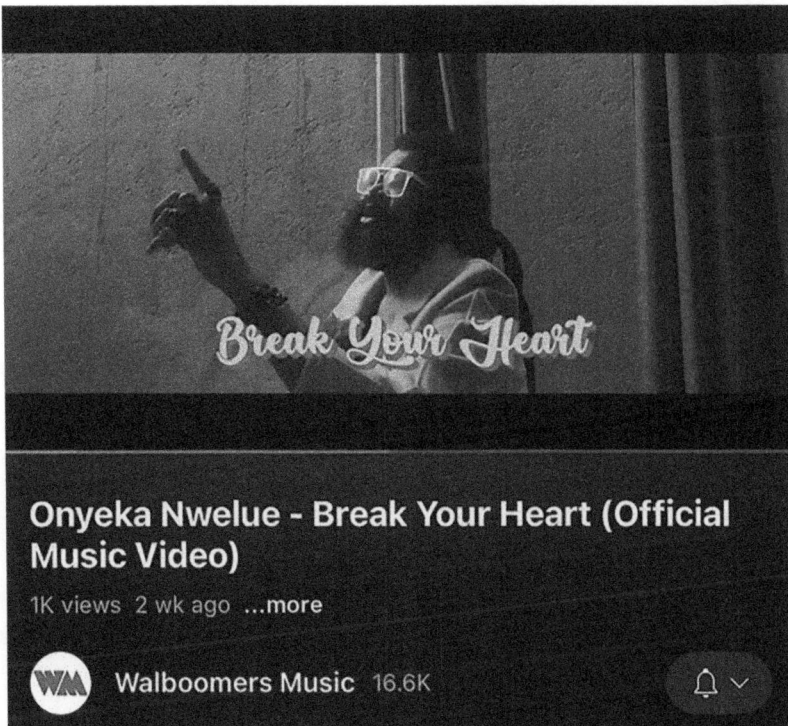

**Onyeka Nwelue - Break Your Heart (Official Music Video)**

1K views  2 wk ago  ...more

WM  Walboomers Music  16.6K

Beyond personal expression, music has been a conduit for cultural preservation and promotion. Through my record label, La Cave Musik, I have aimed to spotlight African musical talents and bring their artistry to a global audience. This endeavour reflects my commitment to celebrating and sustaining the rich musical heritage of the continent.

In my literary and cinematic works, music often plays a central role. For instance, my documentary "The House of Nwapa" not only chronicles the life of Nigeria's first female novelist, Flora Nwapa, but also underscores the significance of cultural expression through music and storytelling.

In essence, music has been an integral thread weaving through the fabric of my life, influencing my creative endeavours, providing solace during adversity, and serving as a bridge connecting diverse cultures and narratives.

At its core, musical magic refers to the extraordinary ability of music to evoke powerful emotions, inspire creativity, and even alter our perceptions. This concept is rooted in the idea that music can tap into a deeper, hidden order of reality, resonating with our souls and revealing symbolic connections between the human experience and the universe.

Over the years, I have come to feel music's magic in many ways:

1. Emotional Resonance: Music's ability to evoke deep emotions and create a sense of connection with others is a hallmark of its magical nature. Whether it's the soaring crescendos of a symphony or the haunting intimacy of a solo piano piece, music has the power to touch our hearts and minds in ways that transcend language.

2. Transformative Power: Music's capacity to transform our moods, emotions, and even our lives is a testament to its magical properties. From the therapeutic benefits of music therapy to the motivational power of anthems and rallying cries, music's impact is multifaceted and profound.

3. Universal Language: Music's ability to bridge cultural divides and speak to fundamental human experiences makes it a universal language, capable of transcending borders and boundaries. Whether it's the rhythmic pulse of African drums or the soaring melodies of Indian ragas, music's diversity is a reflection of its boundless potential.

While music's magical properties may seem intangible, research has shed light on the psychological and neuroscientific mechanisms that underlie its effects. Studies have shown that music can stimulate the brain's reward centres, releasing dopamine and endorphins that enhance our mood and sense of well-being. Additionally, music's ability to evoke emotions and memories is closely tied to its capacity to tap into our brain's default mode network, which is responsible for introspection and self-reflection.

Throughout history, music has been regarded as a form of magic by many cultures and civilizations. From the ancient Greeks to modern-day musicians, the notion that music possesses mystical properties has been a recurring theme. As the renowned musician Jimi Hendrix once described his craft, "completely, utterly a magic science".

In addition to its emotional and therapeutic benefits, music has also played a significant role in social movements and cultural expression. From the civil rights movement to the anti-apartheid movement, music has been a powerful tool for social change, inspiring and mobilizing people around a common cause.

The impact of music on our lives is multifaceted and profound. Music's magical properties are a testament to its enduring power and appeal. Whether we're musicians, music lovers, or simply individuals seeking solace in sound, music's enchanted realm offers a wealth of benefits and experiences waiting to be explored. As Lord Byron, the British poet and politician so eloquently put it, "There's music in all things, if men had ears". This underscores the idea that music is an integral part of our human experience, capable of touching our hearts and minds in ways that transcend language and culture.

As we continue to explore the depths of music's impact on our lives, we may discover even more ways in which it can inspire, heal, and transform us. Whether through its emotional resonance, transformative power, or universal language, music remains a vital part of our shared human experience, offering a wealth of benefits and experiences that can enrich our lives in countless ways.

Life, is a grand symphony where rhythms intertwine with emotions and melodies echo the soul's deepest yearnings, music emerges as the alchemist's stone—transmuting pain into joy, memories into anthems, and dreams into reality. For Davido, music is not merely an art form; it is the very essence of his existence, a magical force that has guided his journey from the bustling streets of Lagos to the global stages of the world.

Davido's musical odyssey began with the release of "Dami Duro" and as his career progressed, he continued to weave intricate tapestries of emotion through his music. Tracks like "If" and "Fall" from his 2019 album A Good Time exemplify his ability to blend heartfelt lyrics with infectious melodies. "Fall," in particular, achieved remarkable success, becoming one of the top-100-most-Shazam-searcRFhed singles in America in January 2019 and the longest-charting Nigerian pop song in Billboard history at the time . These songs are more than just chart-toppers; they are sonic spells that capture the complexities of love and longing.

In 2023, amidst personal trials, Davido released his fourth studio album, Timeless. This album stands as a testament to his resilience and the healing power of music. Blending genres such as amapiano, Afrobeats, and highlife, Timeless received critical acclaim and commercial success, debuting at number 37 on the Billboard 200 chart and breaking streaming records across various platforms . The album's themes of love, loss, and hope resonate deeply, offering listeners a cathartic experience.

Davido's influence extends beyond Nigeria's borders. His collaborations with international artists like Chris Brown on "Blow My Mind" and Victoria Monét on "Offa Me" from his 2025 album 5ive showcase his role as a global conductor, orchestrating cross-cultural musical dialogues. These partnerships not only amplify his reach but also highlight the universal language of music—a language that transcends borders and unites diverse audiences.

Through his artistry, Davido has become a modern-day sorcerer, casting spells that enchant, inspire, and heal. His music is a magical elixir, blending traditional African sounds with contemporary influences to create a unique and captivating sonic experience. Each track is a potion, carefully concocted to evoke emotion, provoke thought, and ignite the soul's fire.

In the realm of music, where magic is real and melodies are spells, Davido stands as a master alchemist. His journey is a testament to the transformative power of music—a force that turns pain into beauty, dreams into reality, and artists into legends. As we listen to his songs, we are reminded that music is not just sound; it is magic incarnate.

Davido's music has profoundly impacted fans worldwide, resonating deeply with their personal experiences and emotions. Many have shared heartfelt testimonies about how his songs have influenced their lives.

In a recent interview, Davido reflected on the overwhelming support he received during a period of inactivity, noting that the music industry felt unusually quiet in his absence. He remarked, "I knew that people loved me because when I was not active, the whole industry shut down. Like I was like, 'Damn, they do love me.' It's so quiet out here. David come back. Even the fans that hate me were like, 'Please come back, we need to diss you...'"

The fervent support for artists like Davido underscores music's profound influence. Fans have expressed how his songs uplift their spirits and offer a sense of connection, illustrating music's role as a unifying and healing force. Their admiration has been expressed through various social media platforms. For instance, a TikTok user shared an emotional tribute, highlighting how Davido's music has been a source of comfort and inspiration during challenging times. Another fan emphasized the unique contribution Davido has made to the music industry, stating that his songs have a distinctive quality that sets them apart.

These testimonies highlight the profound connection between Davido's music and his audience, illustrating how his artistry transcends entertainment to touch the very core of human experience.

# 5
• • • •

# LEADER
# OF HIS
# LEAGUE

In 2013, I invited Davido to Paris. Despite holding a U.S. passport, he required a work visa to perform in France. The U.S. passport, which typically allows for visa-free travel to many countries, couldn't grant Davido unrestricted access , as he encountered a bureaucratic hurdle when he needed to perform professionally in France. As a musician, he required a work visa to legally perform in the country. This situation highlights the complexities of international travel and work regulations, even for individuals with privileged passports. While U.S. passport holders enjoy relatively easy travel to many countries, specific requirements for work visas can vary significantly. In Davido's case, obtaining a work visa for France had involved meeting some specific criteria.

Obtaining a work visa can be time-consuming and may require coordination with French authorities, promoters, or management teams. This experience underscores the importance of understanding visa requirements and planning ahead for international performances. In the entertainment industry, where global tours and collaborations are common, navigating visa regulations is crucial for artists to fulfil their professional commitments. That was where I came in. I facilitated the acquisition of this permit, ensuring that all legal prerequisites were met for his European debut.

This endeavour was more than administrative; it was a bridge between continents, cultures, and artistic expressions. Paris, with its rich history of art and music, provided an ideal backdrop for Davido's introduction to a European audience. The city's vibrant energy and appreciation for diverse musical genres made it a fitting stage for an artist whose sound encapsulates the dynamism of modern Africa. The performance was a resounding success, marking a significant milestone in Davido's rising career. It not only expanded his international footprint but also underscored the universal appeal of Afrobeat music. The Paris show served as a testament to the power of cultural exchange and the unifying force of music.

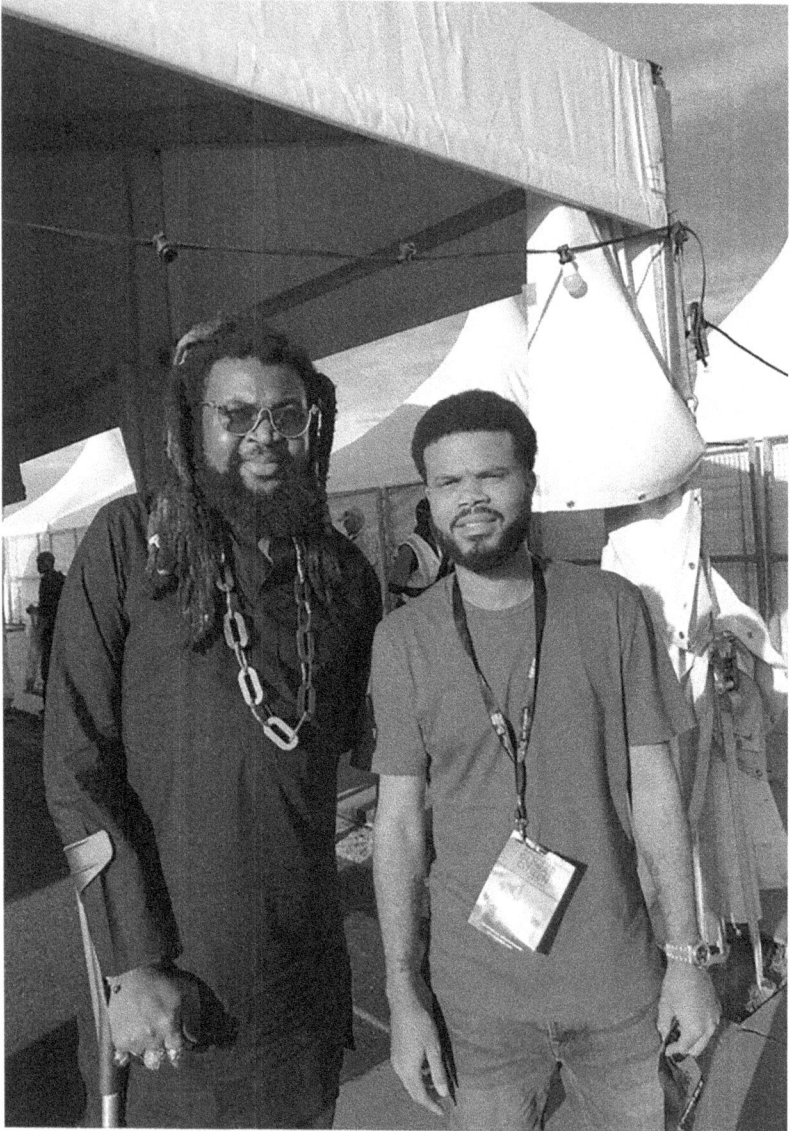

Reflecting on this experience, it's evident that such collaborations and cross-cultural engagements are pivotal in shaping the global music landscape. They foster mutual understanding, celebrate diversity, and pave the way for artists to share their unique narratives with the world. In facilitating Davido's Paris performance, I was reminded of music's profound ability to transcend borders and connect souls. It's a universal language, one that speaks to our shared humanity and collective aspirations.

Davido's impact on the music industry extends beyond his own music. He has been credited with popularizing the Afrobeats genre globally, paving the way for other African artists to break into the international market. His philanthropic efforts have also made a significant impact. He has been involved in various charitable initiatives, including the Davido Foundation, which focuses on providing support to orphaned children and promoting education in Nigeria.

One notable example of Davido's philanthropy is his support for the less privileged.

In 2019, he donated to the victims of the Lagos building collapse, providing financial assistance to those affected. Such acts of kindness have endeared him to his fans and solidified his reputation as a caring and compassionate artist.

Throughout his career, Davido has received numerous awards and accolades. Some of his notable awards include the BET Award for Best International Act (2018), the MOBO Award for Best African Act (2017), The Headies Award for Song of the Year (2018), the AFRIMA Award for Best Male West Africa (2019),among others. These awards are a testament to Davido's hard work and dedication to his craft. He has consistently pushed the boundaries of what is possible in the music industry, and his success has inspired a new generation of artists.

Davido's influence on the music industry is undeniable. His music has been praised for its infectious beats and catchy melodies. His collaborations with international artists have also helped to bridge the gap between African music and the global music industry. His work with artists like Chris Brown and Meek Mill has introduced his music to new audiences, and he has become a sought-after collaborator in the industry. Davido's journey to becoming one of Africa's most successful musicians is a testament to his hard work, dedication, and passion for music. With a career spanning over a decade, Davido has consistently pushed the boundaries of what is possible in the music industry.

As a leader in his league, Davido continues to inspire and entertain fans around the world. His music, philanthropy, and entrepreneurial spirit have made him a true icon in the world of Afrobeats. In the words of Davido himself:

"I'm not just a musician, I'm a movement." Indeed, Davido's impact on the music industry and beyond is undeniable, and his legacy will continue to be felt for years to come.

In my work, I often explore themes of social justice, identity, and personal struggle. I have long been an admirer of Professor Wole Soyinka, Africa's first Nobel Laureate. In fact, I wrote a poem for him, which I presented during the Wole Soyinka Festival when I was just 16 years old. This encounter marked the beginning of a lifelong appreciation for Soyinka's work. I have often spoken about the profound impact Soyinka's life and writings have had on me. Soyinka's resilience and determination are a source of inspiration for me.

Shina Rambo and B-Red were both signed to Davido's record label, Davido Music Worldwide (DMW). Shina Rambo, whose real name is Adeshina Adelekes, is a Nigerian rapper and singer who gained popularity after joining DMW in 2012. B-Red, on the other hand, is a Nigerian singer and rapper who was also a key artist under DMW. Both artists played significant roles in Davido's musical journey, contributing to his success and collaborating on several hit tracks. Shina Rambo's hit single "Shina Rambo" and other songs showcased his talent, while B-Red's vocals and song writing skills were featured in various DMW releases. During their time under DMW, both artists benefited from the label's resources and exposure, which helped them build their fan bases and establish themselves in the Nigerian music industry.

However, both artists eventually parted ways with Davido and DMW. Shina Rambo's departure was marked by a public feud with Davido, with both parties exchanging heated words on social media. The feud seemed to stem from creative differences and possibly financial disputes. B-Red also had a fallout with Davido, which led to his exit from the label. The reasons behind B-Red's departure were less publicly dramatized than Shina Rambo's, but it was clear that the relationship between him and Davido had soured.

Despite their past collaborations, the relationships between Davido and these artists have been strained. The fallouts have been a topic of discussion among fans and industry insiders, with many speculating about the underlying causes. Nevertheless, their time under DMW helped shape their careers and contributed to the Afrobeats scene. Both Shina Rambo and B-Red have continued to pursue their musical endeavours, releasing new music and performing at various events.

The dynamics of their relationships with Davido serve as a reminder of the complexities and challenges that can arise in the music industry, particularly when it comes to artist-label relationships and creative differences. The entertainment industry is known for its competitive nature, and disputes between artists and their labels or management teams are not uncommon. In the cases of Shina Rambo and B-Red, their experiences under DMW and their subsequent departures highlight the importance of clear communication and mutual respect in any professional relationship.

In the aftermath of their departures, both Shina Rambo and B-Red have had to rebuild and redefine their careers. They have done so by focusing on their individual artistry and exploring new musical directions. Shina Rambo, in particular, has been open about his struggles and challenges in the industry, using his platform to share his experiences and offer advice to aspiring artists. B-Red, on the other hand, has continued to release music that showcases his unique style and talent.

The stories of Shina Rambo and B-Red serve as a testament to the ever-changing nature of the music industry. Artists must constantly adapt and evolve to remain relevant, and sometimes, this means navigating complex relationships and making difficult decisions. Despite the challenges they faced, both artists have demonstrated resilience and determination, qualities that are essential for success in the competitive world of music.

However, Shina Rambo and B-Red, despite their public feuds, have shown positive sides to their personalities and careers. Shina Rambo is a talented artist who has showcased his skills as a rapper and singer through various hits. His determination and resilience in his career are evident, as he continues to produce music and perform despite challenges. During his time under DMW, Shina Rambo was loyal to Davido and contributed to the label's success, demonstrating his commitment to his craft. B-Red, on the other hand, is a versatile artist who has explored various musical styles, showcasing his talent as a singer and rapper. He has collaborated with other artists, including Davido, to produce hit tracks and build relationships within the industry. His passion for music is evident in his performances and releases, demonstrating his dedication to his craft.

Both Shina Rambo and B-Red have used their platforms to inspire fans and contribute to the growth of the Afrobeats genre. As Nigerian artists, they have represented their country and showcased their rich musical talent to a global audience. Through their music and performances, they have earned a loyal fan base and made significant contributions to the music industry. Despite their controversies, Shina Rambo and B-Red have demonstrated a commitment to their art and a passion for music that has resonated with fans. Their talents and dedication have earned them a place in the Nigerian music industry, and their contributions to Afrobeats will likely be remembered for years to come.

# 6
. . . .
# UNDERDOGS

I was raised in a family deeply rooted in intellectual and civic engagement, and my early life was imbued with values of service, scholarship, and spiritual discipline. My father, Chukwuemeka Samuel Nwelue, was a respected local politician and community leader, while my mother, Catherine Ona Nwelue, is a dedicated social scientist. This nurturing environment fostered my burgeoning passion for the arts, leading me to explore the realms of writing and filmmaking from a young age. lLike a few other narratives which we'll later come across as this chapter unfolds, my journey from a modest upbringing to international acclaim epitomizes the quintessential underdog story.

Despite the supportive backdrop, my path was fraught with challenges. My decision to pursue a career in the arts, particularly in a society that often prioritizes conventional professions, was met with scepticism. Undeterred, I channelled my experiences into my work, crafting narratives that reflected the complexities of Nigerian society. My debut novel, "The Abyssinian Boy," written during my travels in India, garnered critical acclaim and established me as a formidable literary voice.

My foray into filmmaking further showcased my versatility. My documentary, "The House of Nwapa," paid homage to my aunt, Flora Nwapa, Africa's first female novelist published in English. The film not only celebrated Flora's legacy but also underscored my commitment to preserving African literary heritage.

Central to my journey was the profound relationship I had with Peace Anyiam-Osigwe, the visionary founder of the Africa Movie Academy Awards (AMAA). Peace's unwavering support and mentorship played a pivotal role in my career. It provided me with platforms to showcase my work and navigate the intricacies of the entertainment industry. Her untimely death in January 2023 was a devastating blow. To this day, Peace Anyiam-Osigwe remains one of my greatest losses in life. Her loss was more than personal; it symbolized the departure of a guiding light in my life. Her absence left a void that challenged me to find new sources of inspiration and resilience. It was difficult, but I managed to channel my grief into my art and continued to create works that resonate with authenticity and depth. From the quiet streets of Ezeoke Nsu to the global literary stage, I have managed to carve a niche for myself, inspiring countless others to pursue their dreams against all odds.

Just like me, there are stories of a few others I'd like to share—testaments to resilience, ambition, and the relentless pursuit of dreams. One such story is that of Pascal Chibuike Okechukwu, widely known as Cubana Chief Priest.

Born on April 2, 1981, in Umuhu Okabia,
Orsu Local Government Area of Imo State,
Nigeria, Pascal's early life was marked by
modesty and determination. Raised by his
mother after his father's departure, he grew up
in Aba, Abia State, where he learned the art of
shoemaking—a skill that would later become a
stepping stone in his journey. While studying
at Federal Polytechnic Nekede in Owerri,
Pascal combined his academic pursuits with his
shoemaking business. His dedication paid off
when he earned his first million naira through
this craft, showcasing his entrepreneurial spirit
early on.

Despite an initial aspiration to become
a musician, Pascal found his true calling in
the hospitality and entertainment industry.
He began his career working in small-scale
businesses before joining the Cubana Group,
founded by Obi Cubana. As the General
Manager, he played a pivotal role in managing
nightclubs, lounges, and hotels, including the
renowned Cubana Lounge in Owerri. Pascal's
vibrant personality and ability to connect with
people earned him the moniker "Cubana Chief

Priest." His charisma and networking skills attracted high-profile clientele, solidifying his reputation in Nigeria's nightlife scene.

In 2020, seeking to forge his own path, Pascal parted ways with the Cubana Group and established Club Xhrine in Owerri. This venture marked a significant milestone, allowing him to further expand his influence in the hospitality industry. Beyond his business endeavours, Cubana Chief Priest is known for his philanthropic activities, supporting various causes, including education and community development. His journey from humble beginnings to becoming a prominent figure in Nigeria's entertainment landscape serves as an inspiration to many.

Pascal's story reminds us that underdogs, through resilience and determination, can rise to remarkable heights. His narrative, like mine, underscores the transformative power of ambition and the importance of seizing opportunities to redefine one's destiny.

Another such story is that of Soso Soberekon. Born on June 6 in Port Harcourt, Rivers State, Soso Soberekon hails from Buguma, a town in Nigeria's South-South region. His early life was marked by modest beginnings, but he harboured dreams that soared beyond his immediate environment. As a child, he aspired to become a pilot, often gazing at the skies with wonder, watching airplanes soar overhead. Though that dream didn't materialize, his journey led him to a different kind of stardom.

Soso's foray into the entertainment industry began humbly. He described himself as a "studio rat," spending countless hours in a popular Lagos studio, absorbing the intricacies of music production. His dedication and passion didn't go unnoticed. Through his ability to play the keyboard and his relentless drive, he transitioned from being behind the scenes to becoming a recognized music producer. His big break came when he joined Five Star Music, one of Nigeria's leading record labels, where he served as the general manager. In this role, he worked closely with top Nigerian music acts, contributing significantly to their careers and the label's success.

Despite his achievements, Soso faced challenges. He once missed a life-changing appointment because he didn't have a university degree, a setback that underscored the importance of formal education even in creative industries. This experience motivated him to consider returning to school, emphasizing his commitment to personal growth and development. Beyond his professional life, Soso's personal experiences have also shaped him.

Today, Soso Soberekon is not only a prominent talent manager and producer but also the CEO of White Lion Global. His journey from a studio enthusiast to a key player in Nigeria's entertainment industry exemplifies the underdog narrative—a testament to resilience, adaptability, and the pursuit of excellence.

Deekay is another name that springs to mind. A Nigerian-born Ghanaian artist whose journey in the music industry exemplifies the underdog spirit.

Deekay, born Dennis King-Nanewortor, embarked on his musical journey in 2009 with the release of his debut single, "Gimme Ur Love." Despite his passion and talent, breaking into the competitive Nigerian music scene proved challenging. However, destiny had other plans. In an interview, Deekay recounted how a chance meeting with Davido at a SoundCity event in Ghana became a turning point in his career. They exchanged contacts, and a friendship blossomed. This connection led to their collaboration on the song "High Fever," which became a hit in Ghana and prompted Deekay to relocate to Nigeria to further his music career.

Deekay's association with Davido opened doors, leading to his signing with HKN Music, where he released tracks like "Alele" featuring Mayorkun and Dremo. His versatility in blending Afrobeat, R&B, and rap showcased his unique sound. In 2018, he returned with the single "Hangover," featuring Davido and Peruzzi, reaffirming his place in the industry. Despite facing setbacks, including parting ways with HKN, Deekay's resilience kept him moving forward. He continued to release music independently, demonstrating that determination and passion can sustain a career even amidst challenges. From his early days in Ghana to making waves in Nigeria's music scene, he embodies the underdog spirit—rising against the odds to carve out his own space in the industry.

Tunji Adeleke's story is another one I'd love to share. Affectionately known as "Tungee," his journey from personal trials to public service exemplifies the spirit of an underdog.

Born into the prominent Adeleke family, Tunji is the son of the late Senator Isiaka Adetunji Adeleke, Osun State's first civilian governor. Despite his family's political legacy, Tunji's path was far from straightforward. He faced significant challenges in his academic journey, taking a decade and attending four different universities before finally earning his degree in Business Administration from Adeleke University in 2020. Reflecting on this period, he shared, "Finally! Took me 10 years & 4 Universities!!! Started back in 2010, took breaks in-between for various reasons, completed in 2020. I'm a living testimony, it's not how fast but how well!!!"

Tunji's perseverance extended beyond academics. In 2023, he was appointed Chairman of the Osun State Local Government Service Commission, a role that allowed him to contribute meaningfully to his state's development. His appointment was not merely a nod to his lineage but a recognition of his dedication and capacity to serve. Furthering his commitment to personal growth and public service, Tunji pursued and obtained a master's degree from the University of Hertfordshire. His academic achievements, coupled with his public service, underscore a narrative of resilience and determination.

Tunji Adeleke's story is a testament to the idea that one's background does not solely define their destiny. Through persistence, adaptability, and a commitment to service, he has carved out his own identity, inspiring many who face their own challenges.

Born on October 1, 1960, in Ekeoba village, Umuahia, Abia State, Bright Chimezie Ironmuo, affectionately known as "Okoro Junior," began his musical journey at the tender age of seven. He joined his clan's cultural group and later became a prominent member of the Methodist Church Ekeoba Choir, honing his skills in traditional music and performance. Despite the challenges posed by the Nigerian Civil War, Chimezie pursued his passion for music, leading his school band and collaborating with popular Eastern groups between 1974 and 1979. After completing his secondary education, Chimezie joined the Modernized Odumodu Cultural Dance Group, which specialized in storytelling through music. The group's popularity soared across Eastern Nigeria until its disbandment in 1979. He then joined the Nigerian Customs and Excise Dance Band, touring the country and showcasing his musical talent.

In 1984, Chimezie departed from the Nigerian Customs and Excise Band to form "Zigima," a music group that blended traditional African music with Igbo highlife and captivating dance steps. The term "Zigima" is derived from the Igbo expression "o zi gi ma," meaning "the message that you already know." His debut album, "Respect Africa," featured tracks like "Lekwe Uwa M," "Liza," and "You Can Never Hurry The Sunrise," which resonated with audiences across Nigeria and beyond.

Chimezie's electrifying stage performances took him to countries such as London, Austria, Brazil, and Venezuela, where he represented Nigeria at the OPEC Cultural Festival in Caracas. Notably, he performed for Nelson Mandela during the latter's visit to Nigeria upon his release from prison in 1990, earning admiration from both Mandela and his wife, Winnie.

Despite his success, Chimezie faced challenges in maintaining his musical relevance over the years. However, in April 2025, his classic song "Because of English" experienced a resurgence when Afrobeats superstar Davido publicly credited it as the creative inspiration behind his hit single "With You," featuring Omah Lay. A video of their FaceTime call went viral, with Davido expressing his admiration for Chimezie's work and promising to host him in Lagos. Following Davido's endorsement, "Because of English," originally released in 1984, re-entered public consciousness, debuted on the Spotify Nigeria Top 100 Chart for the first time, decades after its release.

This powerful cycle of influence reinforces the notion that music transcends time, connecting generations and fostering cultural appreciation. When we listen to these revived classics, we should also embrace the ongoing evolution of these musical traditions.

Davido's own journey also mirrors the underdog narrative. Despite being born into affluence, he faced scepticism and criticism in his early career, with many attributing his success to his family's wealth. However, through sheer hard work, perseverance, and dedication to his craft, Davido carved out his own identity in the music industry, earning respect and admiration from peers and fans alike. His recognition of Chimezie's influence underscores his humility and appreciation for the pioneers who paved the way.

In sharing these stories, I want to remind us that success often comes to those who, despite humble beginnings and numerous challenges, remain steadfast in their vision and committed to their goals.

In life's cruel race, we're all underdogs.

# 7

. . .

# THE
# GRAMMYS

As far as artistic accolades are concerned, the Grammy Awards stand as the music industry's equivalent of Mount Olympus—a summit where only the most distinguished are immortalized. Much like the Oscars for film and the Emmys for television, the Grammys have become a symbol of excellence, a golden standard by which musical achievement is measured. For artists, a Grammy win or even a nomination is often seen as the pinnacle of success, a validation of their hard work and dedication to their craft. Their prestige stems from a rigorous selection process, with thousands of industry professionals voting on the year's best works.

This process lends credibility to the awards, making them a benchmark for quality and innovation in music.

The inception of the Grammy Awards dates back to the late 1950s, born from the same cultural renaissance that gave rise to the Hollywood Walk of Fame. As recording executives curated a list of notable figures for the Walk of Fame, they recognized a glaring omission: the music industry lacked its own formal recognition. To address this, they established an award to honour outstanding achievements in the recording arts. The first Grammy Awards ceremony was held on May 4, 1959, simultaneously in Beverly Hills and New York City, presenting 28 awards to artists who had made significant contributions to music in the previous year.

Over the decades, the Grammys have evolved, expanding their categories to reflect the diversity and complexity of the music industry. From classical compositions to contemporary pop hits, the awards have adapted to encompass a broad spectrum of musical genres. The introduction of the "Big Four" categories—

Album of the Year, Record of the Year, Song of the Year, and Best New Artist—has further solidified the Grammys' role as arbiters of musical excellence.

Winning a Grammy has become more than just an honour; it's often a career-defining milestone that can open doors to new opportunities and collaborations. The award epitomizes an artist's talent, hard work, and profound impact on the musical landscape. The Grammys have transformed into a powerful benchmark for success in the music industry. For many artists, a Grammy win embodies the years of unwavering dedication and perseverance they have invested. It represents recognition from peers and industry professionals, affirming their artistic vision and meaningful contributions to music.

The impact of a Grammy win or nomination can be substantial, both for individual artists and the music industry as a whole. A Grammy win can boost an artist's profile, increase their visibility, and even affect their commercial success. For example, artists who win Grammys often see a significant increase in album sales and streaming numbers. Moreover, the Grammys have played a role in shaping the music industry's trends and tastes, influencing what types of music are produced, promoted, and consumed.

Beyond the awards themselves, the Grammys have also become a platform for artists to use their voices and bring attention to important issues. Many artists have used their acceptance speeches to highlight social justice causes, celebrate cultural heritage, or advocate for change within the industry. This aspect of the Grammys adds a layer of depth and meaning to the event, making it more than just a celebration of music but also a forum for expression and activism.

The Grammys' influence extends beyond the music industry, too. The awards show is broadcast globally, reaching millions of viewers and introducing them to new artists and music. This exposure can have a profound impact on an artist's career, helping them reach new audiences and build a global fan base. Furthermore, the Grammys have played a role in shaping popular culture, with many artists using the platform to push boundaries and challenge societal norms.

In essence, the Grammy Awards are more than just trophies; they are symbols of artistic achievement, perseverance, and the relentless pursuit of musical excellence. They stand as a constant reminder to us that while talent is innate, recognition is earned through dedication, innovation, and an unwavering commitment to one's craft.

Africa's rich musical heritage found its first Grammy spotlight in 1966 when South African singer and activist Miriam Makeba, alongside Harry Belafonte, won Best Folk Recording for their album An Evening with Belafonte/Makeba. This win was not just a musical triumph but also a political statement, as Makeba was a vocal opponent of apartheid, using her platform to advocate for social justice.

Over the decades, African artists continued to make their mark. Beninese singer Angélique Kidjo has secured multiple Grammys, celebrating her fusion of African traditions with Western musical elements. Nigerian artists like Burna Boy and Wizkid have also gained international acclaim, with Burna Boy winning Best Global Music Album in 2021 for Twice as Tall.

The Grammy Awards have been a topic of discussion among artists, with some expressing appreciation for the recognition and others criticizing the voting process and lack of diversity. The Weeknd, for instance, boycotted the Grammys in 2020, calling for more transparency in the voting process. He felt that the lack of diversity and representation in the voting body led to biases towards established artists and mainstream genres.

Some have argued that the voting process is opaque and biased towards established artists and mainstream genres. Others point out that certain genres or styles of music are often overlooked or underrepresented.

Some artists have also spoken about the pressure to conform to certain standards in order to be considered for a Grammy. Zach Bryan, for example, refused to submit his latest record for Grammys consideration, citing the pressure to succeed in a system that may not align with his artistic vision. This sentiment is echoed by other artists who feel that the Grammys prioritize popularity over artistic merit. Despite these criticisms, the Grammys remain a significant event in the music industry, with many artists striving for recognition and validation from the Recording Academy.

On the other hand, many artists appreciate the Grammys for the recognition and motivation they provide. n her Best New Artist acceptance speech, Chappell Roan highlighted major issues—like the failure of record labels to provide artists with proper health insurance and fair compensation.. Beyoncé's historic win for Album of the Year for "Cowboy Carter" was a milestone in her career, and she became the first Black woman to receive this honour in the 21st century.

African artists, while not always prominently featured in Grammy discussions, have made significant contributions to global music. While few African artists have publicly expressed opinions on the Grammys, their impact on the music industry is undeniable. Don Jazzy, a Nigerian music producer, has collaborated with international artists, showcasing the growing global influence of African music. The Grammys' recognition of global music, including African genres, has been limited, but there are efforts to increase representation and inclusivity.

The Grammys remain a prestigious award in the music industry, with artists continuing to debate their significance and relevance. While some artists appreciate the recognition, others criticize the voting process and lack of diversity. As the music industry evolves, it will be interesting to see how the Grammys adapt to changing artistic landscapes and global influences.

I want to digress a little to talk about Don Jazzy, a seminal figure in the evolution of contemporary African music, then I'll come back to this discussion.

Don Jazzy, born Michael Collins Ajereh on November 26, 1982, in Umuahia, Abia State, Nigeria, has journeyed from a passionate young musician to an influential producer and entrepreneur underscoring his pivotal role in shaping the Nigerian and global music landscapes.

Raised in Ajegunle, Lagos, Don Jazzy's passion for music was evident from an early age. By 12, he had mastered instruments like the bass guitar and piano. His musical pursuits led him to London in 2000, where he worked various jobs, including as a security guard at McDonald's, while collaborating with artists like JJC Skillz and D'Banj. These experiences laid the foundation for his future endeavours in music production and entrepreneurship.

In 2004, Don Jazzy co-founded Mo' Hits Records with D'Banj, producing numerous hits that defined the Nigerian music scene. Following the label's dissolution, he established Mavin Records in 2012, which became a powerhouse, nurturing talents like Tiwa Savage, Rema, Ayra Starr, and Johnny Drille. Don Jazzy has been instrumental in bridging Nigerian and American music industries. His production work and collaborations have introduced Nigerian sounds to international audiences, fostering cross-cultural musical exchanges. Notably, his involvement in tracks like "Gucci Gang" with D'Prince and Davido exemplifies this fusion.

Don Jazzy's influence extends to artists like Davido, who has cited him as an inspiration in his musical journey. Their collaborations and mutual respect have contributed to the growth and global recognition of Afrobeats. Davido once collaborated with Don Jazzy on a song called "Gentleman" alongside D'Prince. This song was produced by Don Jazzy and features a semi-fast-paced beat, making it suitable for Nigerian wedding settings. The video for

"Gentleman" was directed by Clarence Peters and styled by Okunoren Twins.

Beyond his production accolades, Don Jazzy was honoured as Africa's Most Creative Music Producer of the Year in 2024 in the United States, highlighting his impact on the continent's music industry. While Don Jazzy has not secured a Grammy nomination, he has expressed a pragmatic view regarding such accolades, emphasizing the importance of artistic integrity over awards. In a 2015 interview, he remarked, "I don't think I'll ever win a Grammy... I'm doing perfect, I'm doing great, I don't have big eyes."

Don Jazzy's legacy is not solely defined by awards but by his enduring contributions to music, mentorship of emerging artists, and role in elevating Nigerian music on the global stage.

Now, back to business.

Recognizing the growing global influence of African music, the Recording Academy introduced the Best African Music Performance category in 2024. This category honours quality vocal or instrumental African music recordings, highlighting the continent's diverse musical expressions. South African singer Tyla made history by winning the inaugural award for her hit song "Water," marking a significant milestone in Grammy history.

Davido, a prominent figure in the Afrobeats scene, has been instrumental in bringing African music to the global stage. His album Timeless received multiple Grammy nominations, including Best Global Music Album and Best African Music Performance for the track "Unavailable." These nominations underscore his dedication to his craft and his role in elevating African music worldwide.

The inclusion of African artists and categories in the Grammy Awards reflects a broader recognition of the continent's cultural and musical contributions. As African rhythms continue to influence global music trends, the Grammys serve as a platform celebrating this rich blend of sounds.

As the music industry continues to evolve, the Grammys will likely remain a major force in shaping the sound, style, and direction of music for years to come, now enriched by the vibrant and diverse voices of Africa.

Davido's Grammy journey has been quite notable, with the Nigerian singer receiving three nominations. His album, "Timeless" was nominated in the Best Global Music Album category in 2024. His song, "Unavailable" featuring Musa Keys was nominated in the Best African Music Performance category in 2024. His song, "Feel" was nominated in the Best Global Music Performance category in 2024. He was also nominated as a featured artist on "11:11," which is up for Best R&B Album at the upcoming 2025 Grammy Awards.

Although Davido hasn't won a Grammy Award yet, his consistent nominations showcase his growing global influence and recognition within the music industry. With his upcoming nomination for "11:11" in the Best R&B Album category, Davido's prospects remain bright.

It's worth noting that Davido's success extends beyond the Grammys, with numerous awards and nominations from other prestigious platforms like the BET Awards, MTV Africa Music Awards, and African Muzik Magazine Awards.

# 8
. . . .

# LIFESTYLE

Even with the high cost of living, the luxury lifestyle never ends for Davido.

The allure of celebrity life has long fascinated the public. From high-profile red-carpet events to extravagant vacations, the lifestyles of the affluent and famous often appear to be an endless cycle of excitement and luxury. Their residences are typically expansive estates located in exclusive neighbourhoods, featuring amenities such as opulent swimming pools, state-of-the-art fitness centres, private screening rooms, and personal spas. Additionally, fashion and style are integral aspects of their lives, with celebrities frequently showcasing the latest designer collections and emerging as fashion icons. Travel is another hallmark, with private jets and yachts enabling stars to traverse the globe in comfort and style.

However, behind the façade of glamour lies a more nuanced reality. The relentless media scrutiny, the presence of paparazzi, and the invasion of privacy can profoundly affect even the most seasoned individuals in the spotlight. The need to maintain a public persona amidst overwhelming expectations can create significant pressure. Some celebrities, such as Shaquille O'Neal, have expressed a desire to distance themselves from the "celebrity" label, advocating for a grounded approach and critiquing the superficiality often associated with fame.

In this intricate balance between public perception and personal experience, celebrities navigate a lifestyle that is as demanding as it is captivating. While their lives may appear enviable, they also illustrate the complexities of fame and the universal human yearning for connection and authenticity.

Davido epitomizes the modern celebrity lifestyle with remarkable elegance. Born into privilege, he has transcended his affluent beginnings to carve out a unique identity in the music industry, seamlessly merging his inherited wealth with his own significant achievements. This combination has enabled him to cultivate a lifestyle that's not only lavish but also profoundly influential.

Davido's passion for luxury automobiles is nothing short of impressive. His car collection showcases his refined taste and appreciation for the finer things in life, featuring stunning models like the Rolls-Royce Cullinan, Bentley Bentayga, Lamborghini Huracán, and an array of Mercedes-Benz vehicles. Each of these magnificent cars serves as more than just a mode of transport; they symbolize his elevatedremarkable status and success, prominently displayed in his music videos and social media posts. This further cements his image as a true trendsetter in the entertainment industry.

In his downtime, Davido can often be found frequenting high-end clubs and lounges, both in Nigeria and across the globe. His presence at these venues elevates ordinary nights into extraordinary events, attracting fans and fellow celebrities alike. Beyond the vibrant nightlife, he enjoys breath-taking vacations, frequently sharing snapshots of his adventures in exotic locations, all while indulging in luxurious accommodations and experiences. Truly, Davido embodies a lifestyle that many admire and aspire to emulate.

Davido's personal life, particularly his relationships, has been a subject of public interest. His engagement and subsequent marriage to Chioma Rowland garnered significant media attention, especially following the tragic loss of their son in 2022. The couple's journey, marked by both joy and sorrow, has been shared with fans, reflecting the human side of celebrity life.

A fashion icon in his own right, Davido's style is a blend of streetwear and high fashion. His wardrobe features pieces from renowned designers, and he often collaborates with fashion brands, further solidifying his influence in the fashion industry. His endorsement deals with companies like Puma and Martell

Cognac not only showcase his marketability but also his ability to bridge the gap between music and lifestyle branding. His journey through the world of brand endorsements tells of his influence and versatility as an artist and entrepreneur. From his early days in the music industry to his current status as a global Afrobeats ambassador, Davido has collaborated with a diverse array of brands, reflecting his broad appeal and business acumen.

At just 17, Davido secured his first major endorsement deal with MTN Nigeria, reportedly worth ₦20 million. This early partnership marked the beginning of his long-standing relationship with major brands.. Over the years, Davido's endorsement portfolio has grown to include several high-profile collaborations, and the impressive list of endorsement deals showcases his marketability and influence across various industries. One of his notable partnerships is with Guinness Nigeria, which began in 2013 when he performed at the Guinness World of More Concert alongside other top Nigerian artists. This collaboration not only highlighted his musical prowess but also cemented his status as a prominent figure in the entertainment industry.

In 2016, Davido became a brand ambassador for Pepsi, further solidifying his presence in the beverage industry. This partnership allowed him to reach a broader audience and reinforce his appeal as a youthful and vibrant brand ambassador. His subsequent endorsement deal with Infinix Mobile in 2018 aligned with the tech industry's growth in Africa, demonstrating his ability to adapt to emerging trends.

In 2021, Davido's endorsement portfolio expanded significantly. He became an ambassador for 1xBet, an international sports betting company, showcasing his appeal in the sports and gaming sectors. Additionally, he partnered with Martell Cognac in a deal reportedly valued at over $5 million, marking one of the most significant endorsement deals in Africa. This partnership not only highlighted his luxurious lifestyle but also reinforced his status as a high-end brand ambassador.

Davido's collaborations continued to diversify in 2021. He became a global brand ambassador for Puma, expanding his influence in the fashion and sportswear industry. He also partnered with Wema Bank's digital platform, ALAT, reflecting his connection with digital innovation and finance. Furthermore, he was unveiled as the first-ever brand ambassador for the snack brand Munch It, tapping into the FMCG sector. His partnership with Viva Plus Laundry Sanitizer detergent powder showcased his versatility in endorsing household products.

The impact of these endorsement deals on Davido's career cannot be overstated. They have not only increased his visibility and reach but also reinforced his status as a marketable and influential celebrity. By partnering with various brands, Davido has been able to leverage his influence and appeal to different audiences, further solidifying his position in the entertainment industry.

In 2024, Davido announced a new partnership with GAC Motors, further diversifying his endorsement portfolio. This collaboration highlights his ability to adapt to different industries and reinforce his marketability. With these endorsement deals, Davido has solidified his status as one of the most influential and sought-after celebrities in Africa, with a brand portfolio that spans multiple industries and sectors. His ability to leverage his influence and appeal to various audiences has made him a valuable partner for brands looking to tap into the African market.

The success of Davido's endorsement deals can be attributed to his authenticity and relatability. As a popular and influential artist, he has built a massive following across Africa and beyond. His endorsement deals are often seen as a reflection of his personal preferences and interests, which resonates with his fans. By partnering with brands that align with his values and image, Davido has been able to create a cohesive and effective marketing strategy that benefits both himself and the brands he works with.

Overall, Davido's endorsement deals have played a significant role in shaping his career and reinforcing his status as a leading celebrity in Africa. His ability to adapt to different industries and leverage his influence has made him a valuable partner for brands looking to tap into the African market. As he continues to expand his endorsement portfolio, it will be interesting to see how he navigates the ever-changing landscape of celebrity endorsements and brand partnerships.

In addition to the aforementioned partnerships, Davido has also collaborated with brands like AXE, Travelbeta, Pennek, and Bitsika, among others. These collaborations span various industries, including grooming, travel, real estate, and fintech, highlighting his broad market appeal. His strategic brand partnerships have not only enhanced his personal brand but have also played a significant role in promoting Nigerian and African culture on the global stage. His ability to align with diverse brands underscores his status as one of Africa's most influential artists.

Davido's embrace of the private jet lifestyle epitomizes his ascent from a budding artist to a global Afrobeats icon. In April 2024, he unveiled his acquisition of a brand-new Bombardier Global 7500 jet, a pinnacle of luxury in private aviation. This aircraft, renowned for its unparalleled range and opulence, reportedly cost between $73 million and $78 million. The

Bombardier Global 7500 boasts four expansive living spaces, a full-size kitchen, and a dedicated crew suite, accommodating up to 14 passengers. Its impressive range allows for non-stop flights of up to 17 hours, connecting continents without the need for layovers. Davido's choice reflects not just a preference for luxury but also a strategic move to facilitate his international engagements and tours.

The sheer opulence of the Bombardier Global 7500 is a testament to Davido's refined taste and appreciation for the finer things in life. Beyond the aircraft's specifications, Davido often shares glimpses of his jet-set lifestyle on social media, showcasing moments of relaxation and work aboard his jet. These insights offer fans a window into the life of an artist who seamlessly blends business with pleasure, using his private jet as both a mode of transport and a mobile hub for creativity and collaboration. The investment in a high-calibre aircraft clearly illustrates his significant status in the music industry and highlights his commitment to establishing a global presence.

Davido's influence extends far beyond his music. He is a true icon, inspiring countless fans around the world with his success story. His ability to blend luxury, influence, and social responsibility is a hallmark of his character, setting a benchmark for aspiring artists and public figures. Beyond the glitz, Davido is known for his philanthropic efforts. He has contributed to various charitable causes, including donations to orphanages and support for education initiatives. His influence extends beyond entertainment, as he often uses his platform to advocate for social issues and inspire his fans to give back to their communities.

The impact of Davido's success story cannot be overstated. He is a shining example of what can be achieved through hard work, dedication, and a passion for one's craft. His commitment to excellence is evident in every aspect of his career, from his music to his fashion sense. Davido's style is a fusion of African elegance and global sophistication, making him a trendsetter in the entertainment industry. His ability to connect with fans from diverse backgrounds is a testament to his broad appeal and influence.

As a global Afrobeats icon, Davido is paving the way for other African artists to break into the international market. His success serves as an encouraging example of the opportunities available to talented artists who are willing to put in the effort to achieve their goals. Davido's vision for advancing opportunities for African artists on the world stage is inspiring, and his commitment to using his platform for good is truly admirable. In essence, Davido's lifestyle is a blend of inherited privilege and personal accomplishment. He embodies the modern celebrity who seamlessly integrates luxury, influence, and social responsibility, setting a benchmark for aspiring artists and public figures.

Davido's legacy extends beyond his music and fashion sense. He is a role model for young artists and fans around the world, showing them that success is within reach with hard work and determination. His philanthropic efforts and commitment to social responsibility are an inspiration to many, and his influence will undoubtedly be felt for generations to come. As he continues to soar to new heights, both literally and figuratively, Davido remains a true icon in the entertainment industry, and his impact will be remembered for years to come.

# 9
. . . .
# LIFETIME

A lifetime is a grand journey—an odyssey of moments that define who we are, marked by our triumphs, trials, and the legacy we leave behind. For many, it's a map of peaks and valleys; for others, a melody of beginnings, pauses, reinventions. This chapter casts my own lifetime, along with Davido's—its vibrant notes and silent undertones—into perspective, capturing the tapestry of a life in tandem with ambition, adversity, and artistry.

As detailed in the earlier pages, I hail from a family steeped in civic engagement, storytelling, and intellect. My father, the late Chukwuemeka Samuel Nwelue, served as a local politician;

my mother, Catherine Ona Nwelue, is a social scientist, and my aunt, Professor Leslye Obiora, served as Nigeria's Minister of Mines and Steel. As a child, I organized moonlight storytelling sessions and self-funded tutorial clubs at boarding school—my earliest attempts at blending the literary with the communal spirit of Imo land.

By 16, I was immersed in Lagos's cultural circuits, meeting literary giants like Wole Soyinka and Beautiful Nubia, and publishing my first novel, The Abyssinian Boy. Completed in India, the novel won the TM Aluko Prize, was runner-up for the Ibrahim Tahir Prize, and earned a ₦2.5 million advance. This debut paved the way for becoming the first African member of Sandbox, a global community of innovators under 30.

Subsequent works, including Burnt and Hip-Hop Is Only for Children, garnered critical acclaim. Burnt earned praise from poet George Szirtes and toured 25 European countries, translated into several languages. Meanwhile, Hip-Hop Is Only for Children won BEST Creative Non-Fiction Book in 2015.

I ventured into film with The House of Nwapa, a documentary celebrating Flora Nwapa, Africa's first female novelist. The film was showcased at over a dozen festivals and shortlisted for Best Documentary at the 2017 Africa Movie Academy Awards. Following that, I wrote and directed Agwaetiti Obiụtọ, which earned AMAA shortlist honours and festival acclaim (vanguardngr.com).

My academic path led me to Oxford as an Academic Visitor in 2021. My claims of being a professor at Oxford and Cambridge were later retracted, resulting in termination for misuse of titles—an experience that exposed the tensions between ambition and integrity. I apologized and appealed, acknowledging the missteps while reflecting on institutional expectations and self-representation.

Driven by legacy, I established the James Currey Society in 2019, along with a prize (£1,000) to reward emerging African fiction writers via the James Currey Prize. I also founded Abibiman Publishing and co-founded La Cave Musik, aiming to amplify African creative voices across media.

I lectured at institutions like the University of Hong Kong, University of Lagos, and Ohio University—without remuneration—driven by a passion for knowledge-sharing. In 2022, I was appointed Haiti's Honorary Consul to Anglophone West Africa—a first in Haiti's history.

Life's path has not been without hardship. A car accident in 2018 confined me to a wheelchair for months . The Oxford/Cambridge fallout was deeply painful. But in these valleys I found resilience, transforming setbacks into lessons and deepening my artistic resolve.

I divide my time between South Africa, the UK, and Nigeria, weaving a life across continents. I hold an honorary Doctor of Humane Letters from Université du Québec in Haiti . My work has been featured in The Guardian, Farafina, and others. Despite controversy, I continue self-publishing over 20 titles and managing a multimedia consultancy that organizes global literary and music festivals.

My lifetime until now reads like a novel: early promise, notable acclaim, sudden adversity, personal accountability, resurgence, and global initiatives. I have always believed that a 'lifetime' must be marked by contributions, not only to self but to collective imagination—be it through novels, films, scholarships, or dialogues across borders. I stand today with humility and aspiration, aware of my human flaws and my potential legacy. My story is unfinished— each book, festival, talk, and collaboration is a continuation of that journey.

In the arc of a lifetime, the past informs the present, and the present writes the future. As I continue to navigate the unpredictability of creativity, culture, and community, I remain committed to storytelling that transcends boundaries, to telling stories that are woven from triumphs, trials, aspirations, and the moments that define us. In reflecting on my own life—from a small town in Imo State to global stages—it becomes clear that my journey mirrors the arc of others, none more so than Davido's. Both our lives illuminate a shared truth: nothing worth achieving comes on a platter.

Davido's personal life has been a subject of fascination for many, with his relationships, children, and experiences shaping him into the man he is today. As a father of six, with three boys and three girls across multiple partners, Davido's journey of parenthood has been marked by both joy and heartbreak. His first daughter, Aurora Imade Adeleke, was born on May 22, 2015, to Sophia Momodu, and their relationship sparked a custody battle after a disputed DNA test. Despite the challenges, Davido has publicly committed to being a devoted father, and he and Sophia have since reached a respectful co-parenting arrangement.

Davido's relationship with Amanda, also known as Laplubelle, resulted in the birth of their daughter, Hailey Veronica Adeleke, on May 9, 2017. Although their relationship was short-lived, they have maintained friendly co-parenting dynamics, with Davido even gifting Amanda a Porsche worth approximately ₦35 million. Another significant relationship in Davido's life is with Chioma Avril Rowland, whom he met at Babcock University. Their romance spans back to 2015, and they have a son, David Ifeanyi Adeleke Jr., born on October 20, 2019. Tragically, Ifeanyi drowned in their

Banana Island home on October 31, 2022, triggering a police investigation and prompting Davido to take a temporary break from public life. The loss of Ifeanyi was a turning point in Davido's life, and it had a profound impact on his artistic direction. He channelled his grief into his music, resulting in the emotionally rich albums Timeless and 5ive. Davido and Chioma's relationship was put to the test after Ifeanyi's death, but they eventually got married in March 2023, and welcomed twins, a boy and a girl, later that year.

Yet, Davido's personal life has also faced its share of controversy.. In 2013, Ayotomide Labinjo claimed that Davido fathered a child with her, but a DNA test came back negative, dispelling the allegations. In 2017, Larissa Lorenco gave birth to a son named Dawson, and a DNA test confirmed Davido's paternity. Additionally, in 2023, Anita Brown and Ivanna Bay alleged that they were pregnant with Davido's children, although these claims remain unverified.

Despite the scrutiny and challenges, Davido has consistently declared his children as blessings and has demonstrated a commitment to being a responsible father. His relationships with the mothers of his children, including Sophia Momodu and Amanda, have been subject to public scrutiny, but he has maintained a level of respect and cooperation in co-parenting.

Throughout his personal life, Davido has shown resilience and a capacity for growth. His experiences, though marked by heartbreak and controversy, have shaped him into a devoted father and partner. As he navigates the complexities of celebrity parenthood, Davido's story serves as a reminder that behind every public figure lies a deeply human story of joy, sorrow, responsibility, and the enduring power of love and fatherhood. Despite the ups and downs, Davido's relationships and experiences have ultimately contributed to his growth as a person and an artist, and his music continues to reflect the depth of his emotions and the complexity of his life.

For me, the path from Ezeoke Nsu to literary acclaim was paved with doubt and determination. Similarly, Davido faced widespread scepticism in his early days. As he shared in a Streetz94.5 interview, "lots of people didn't believe" in his career choice. Many assumed his wealth was the key, but as he told Business Untitled, "the biggest challenge ... was that my father is wealthy. But I got accepted for one reason ... I am good, talented". We both discovered that talent, perseverance, and values—not privilege—forge resilience and success.

I grappled with prestige, controversy, and personal loss. Davido faced his own crucible— he battled impostor syndrome, confessing, "If I always felt like ... I'm Davido everything I record will enter, I'd fall ... I record like it's my first song every time". That humility echoed my own ethos: every story, speech, and film is crafted anew, with fresh intention and respect for my craft.

I lost mentors, confronted academic setbacks, and endured public scrutiny. Davido endured tragedy too—losing his son Ifeanyi. As he told CNN, he withdrew from public life until the outpouring of support reminded him "you're fine... everybody is rooting for you". In parallel, Peace Anyiam-Osigwe's passing shook me deeply, showing how love and grief shape our courage to create.

My story involves controversy and acclaim; Davido's life has been no less complex. He revealed how fame affected his family—his daughter was bullied, his father confronted rumours, and relatives had to switch schools because of his celebrity. That same fame was once deemed a liability; in fact, Davido's father reportedly cancelled shows and obstructed promotions early on. Yet he persevered, just as I did through the Oxford–Cambridge debacle— emerging more resolved, more committed to authenticity.

I've lectured internationally, built publishing houses, and championed African voices. Davido has paralleled this arc—signing with Sony and RCA, yet returning to Lagos to create hits like "If" and "Fall", which showed the world the core of his artistry, not just the shine of a contract. He navigates fame and criticism— some dismiss his videos as "wack," others mock him online, but he remains unbreakable: "it's just bants to me".

Our lives—though in different arenas—share a common narrative: we were both underdogs. We worked tirelessly, fell hard, learned the value of support, and found clarity in adversity. We stood tall in the face of scepticism and rose precisely because of the resolve it cultivated. As I reflect on my own lifetime, its milestones and missteps—literary awards, festival screenings, global dialogues—I see in Davido's journey the same heartbeat: resilience, reinvention, and relentless passion.

In the end, our stories remind us: nothing worthwhile is given; it's earned in quiet sacrifice, public scrutiny, and private resolve. Our narratives are not isolated—they are chords in a grander anthem.

This chapter closes, but the lifetime is still being written.

# 10

· · · · · ·

# Love for an Uncle, Love of an Uncle

ONYEKA NWELUE

Love is a flame that flickers with fervent passion, a gentle breeze that whispers sweet nothings, and a canvas painted with the vibrant hues of the human experience. Like Cupid's arrow, love pierces the heart, igniting a fire that burns brightly, yet can also leave scars that linger long after the flame has extinguished.

As the poet Maya Angelou once wrote, "Love recognizes no barriers. It jumps over them all." Love is a force that transcends borders, defies conventions, and bridges the gaps between individuals. It is a symphony of emotions, a harmony of heartbeats, and a dance of souls. Like a rose in full bloom, love is beautiful, yet fragile. It requires nurturing, care, and attention to flourish. As the ancient Greeks knew, love comes in many forms – eros, philia, storge, and agape – each a unique manifestation of the human heart's capacity to love.

In the grand scheme of things, love is the thread that weaves together moments of joy, sorrow, triumph, and heartbreak. It is the whispered promise in the dead of night, the gentle touch that soothes the soul, and the warmth that chases away the darkness. As we embark on this journey to explore the mysteries of love, let us navigate the twists and turns of the human heart, and uncover the secrets that make love a universal language, spoken by all, yet understood by each in their own way.

My relationship with Peace was more than mentorship—it was familial. She was the aunt I never had and the compass I didn't know I needed. Her early support transformed my trajectory: in 2012, under her aegis at the Africa Film Academy, she enabled my studies at Prague Film School. That gesture unlocked a new horizon for me. Her devotion transcended mere encouragement—it reshaped my life's contours. When Peace passed, it felt like losing a limb. I found myself void and lost. Peace Anyiam-Osigwe's death took everything from me ... I made a video in Oxford just before she died ... she remains one of my greatest losses in life. The grief was debilitating—a deep pool of sorrow that shook my spirit. As I have previously written, her absence taught me not to take life too seriously, turning me subtly toward a calmer, prayerful acceptance. Peace's unwavering belief prepared me for challenges I had not yet imagined—festivals, films, literary initiatives.

Just as my bond with Peace was rooted in shared purpose and affection, Davido's life is anchored in family values—an unshakeable foundation that sustains him amid the limelight. His reputation as a devoted son and brother is well-known. Born the youngest of five, he often speaks warmly about family dinners and holidays, nurturing traditions even as his globe-trotting career demands time and travel. He customarily includes siblings in both business and personal milestones, ensuring that his rise is shared, not solitary.

Davido and Chioma's journey together began in 2013 at Babcock University, with Davido's manager Lati facilitating their meeting. Over eight years, their love story weathered highs, lows, cheating rumours, and a breakup in early 2021 following reports of Davido's liaison with other women, including Larissa – the scandal shook many. Despite their split, co-parenting remained steady. In January 2022, Davido and Chioma were spotted together at a family gathering – a quiet reconciliation that set the tone for healing. Their reunification continued in church, public events, and even night-outs— Davido sporting the "002" necklace, a visible symbol of their restored bond.

By mid-2023, Davido opened up on the ABTalks podcast, calling his fallout with Chioma the moment he "let himself down" and affirming that "he has fixed it". In March 2023 he officially wed her, and by June 2024 they tied the knot traditionally, a testament to enduring partnership. Humility and intention define their parenting dynamic. Davido explained the balancing act: "love for the kids comes first... their mums are good people and my friends".

Shared schedules, school runs, birthdays, and even church services reflect a deliberately co-parenting model—unity rooted in love.

Their relationship trajectory—from public breakup to renewed affection—reveals both emotional intelligence and growth. The once highly publicized drama faded, replaced by intentionality: at Davido's concert Chioma wore his gold pendant; at family events, she sat beside him, a visible partner once more. Even Davido's dad and siblings have embraced Chioma, reinforcing the family circle's strength.

Davido's nurturing of relationships mirrors mine: like Peace, Chioma supports quietly—managing family spaces and stabilizing shared grief. His approach—repairing, reaffirming, recommitting—embodies family love as cyclical: it fractures, mends, grows stronger. By embracing forgiveness and making conscious efforts to rebuild trust, Davido has elevated love from mere sentiment to life philosophy. His resilience reflects deeply held values: humility, accountability, and unwavering support for the ones who matter most.

In our stories—his and mine—family is not background; it is the stage. It is where love is tested, transformed, and ultimately triumphant.

As we read on, we pause to celebrate not just achievement, but the heart behind the music—family. Now, let's explore the bond between Davido and his beloved dancing uncle.

In the Adeleke family, rhythm isn't just in their music—it's in their very being. This was never more evident than in the figure of Davido's uncle, Senator Ademola Adeleke, often called the "Dancing Senator." His spontaneous, joy-filled moves at official events have become legendary, even earning him the title of the most animated dancer in Nigeria's Senate. Davido immortalized this familial flair in the lyrics of "Owonikoko," singing:

"Ewa bami mujo, ijo baba Sina Rambo" — "Come and dance with me, the dance of Sina Rambo's dad". He later explained, playfully referring to his uncle as "the Nigerian Michael Jackson," in reference to his sleek footwork.

Senator Ademola Adeleke's life stands as a living testament to the power of family, music, and politics. Born on May 13, 1960, in Enugu State to a Yoruba-Muslim father, former Senator Raji Ayoola Adeleke, and an Igbo-Christian mother, Nnena Esther Adeleke, Ademola was destined to bridge cultures. Raised in a politically engaged household, his brother Isiaka Adeleke was Osun's first civilian governor, and his father was a prominent labor leader and senator. Ademola's educational background includes studying at Jacksonville State University and earning a BSc in Criminal Justice from Atlanta Metropolitan State College in 2021.

Ademola's political career took off when he served as Senator for Osun West from 2017 to 2019, taking over the seat after his late brother Isiaka. He later became the Governor of Osun State in July 2022 under the PDP, defeating the incumbent in a high-stakes battle. Notably, his campaign was backed by celebrity rallies, most notably by his nephew Davido. This relationship is rooted in support and inspiration, with Davido rescheduling tours to campaign for Ademola in Osun in both 2018 and 2022.

The "Dancing Senator" moniker suits Ademola perfectly, as he embraces dance as both personal joy and political signature. He describes dance as exhilarating exercise, saying, "my kids got it from me... they will tell me 'we can't catch up with you'". His dance moves at rallies, family celebrations, and public functions, including joint performances with Davido, have become viral symbols of joyful familial unity.

As a paternal uncle to Davido, Ademola has had a significant influence on the musician's artistry and public charm. Davido has repeatedly credited Ademola's zest and musical energy as foundational to his own success.

Ademola's children are following in his rhythmic footsteps. B-Red, born July 23, 1990, in Atlanta, started his music career in 2013 with "Insane Girl" featuring Davido. Shina "Sina Rambo" Adeleke is also a recording artist with hits like "Earthquake" and "Lamborghini". Adenike Adeleke, admired for her vibrant dancing alongside her father, received a Mercedes-Benz as a graduation gift from Oakwood University in 2020. Other children include Nike, Ayootola, Goke, and Folasade, completing a family both musically inclined and politically active.

Senator Ademola Adeleke's legacy is one of joyful leadership and cultural vibrancy. As a cultural ambassador, musical patriarch, and political figure, he has shaped a narrative of unity. Through dance, politics, and familial warmth, Ademola has become a symbol of tradition and modernity, resonating in Davido's music, persona, and public spirit. Ultimately, the Adeleke family's kinship, dances, support, and love define their legacy.

Public displays of their kinship have warmed hearts for years. In 2018, videos surfaced of the Senator dancing at a celebratory election victory event—Davido beside him, both beaming with unfiltered joy. Those dances weren't mere performance—they were shared celebration. Fast forward to 2020 and beyond: clips from Davido's wedding show him prostrating before his uncle (a traditional sign of deep respect), before launching into a spontaneous dance routine together—two generations united in rhythm and reverence. Their bond is inseparable from both celebration and support. From dancing at weddings to trekking campaign rallies—Davido has even campaigned aggressively for his uncle's political campaigns in Osun State, donning PDP agbada and facing close calls, only to earn heartfelt gratitude from supporters and trending online for standing by family.

In May 2024, on Senate Governor Ademola Adeleke's 64th birthday, Davido posted a tender tribute: "Happy Birthday to The Asiwaju Of Edeland... My Uncle, My Bloodline... I love you so much Unc!!! WE NEVER GAVE UP!"

Once again, they danced. Once again, the internet swooned. Fans were reminded of the genuine love and respect that binds the Adelekes—not only through blood but through shared rhythm and joy.

Why do these moments matter? They illustrate that Davido's fame is never solitary— it's woven into a family fabric where love, respect, and shared delight form the bedrock of his identity. The image of Davido and his uncle dancing together—it's more than a meme. It's an intergenerational legacy, reminding us all that even the brightest spotlight doesn't shine brighter than the love that greets us at home.

All through allwe have come to know of Davido's life and career, his dancing uncle and the family bond they share are a steady heartbeat—proof that no star truly outshines the ties that ground them. Family isn't a feature—it's the framework. And through every beat, every performance, every moment together in motion, Davido reminds us that behind every global rhythm is a family that dances with him, for him, and because of him.

www.ingramcontent.com/pod-product-compliance
Lightning Source LLC
Chambersburg PA
CBHW030831090426
42737CB00009B/964